T0291310

Creating Business and Corporate Strategy

Businesses need strategies that determine the direction of functioning and further development. If a company deals with several multifaceted businesses, each of them subsequently requires their own strategy. The issue of strategy creation and realization is a key factor that must receive the closest possible attention.

In order to assure victory and be thoroughly prepared for various directions and situations that may arise, companies create their own unique strategies. This book is primarily aimed at suggesting the necessary repertoire of knowledge and skills for strategy creating with the help of the TASGRAM integrated system – Thinking, Analyzing, Strategy, Goals, Risks, Actions, and Monitoring. The main outcome of TASGRAM is a combined strategic table: business strategy, corporate strategy, goals, risks, actions, and monitoring. Each element in TASGRAM has a concrete goal and it helps users become more focused. *Creating Business and Corporate Strategy: An Integrated Strategic System* offers a new tool for company strategy creation, showcasing various cases and examples based on theory and practice.

Unlike the existing tools, the suggested system of strategy creation is simpler and definite. Its main purpose is to help create and further develop the created strategy, making this book especially valuable to researchers, academics, practitioners, and students in the fields of strategy, leadership, and management.

Adyl Aliekperov, MBA, is a leadership and customer-centered strategy consultant and published author.

Routledge Focus on Business and Management

The fields of business and management have grown exponentially as areas of research and education. This growth presents challenges for readers trying to keep up with the latest important insights. *Routledge Focus on Business and Management* presents small books on big topics and how they intersect with the world of business research.

Individually, each title in the series provides coverage of a key academic topic, whilst collectively, the series forms a comprehensive collection across the business disciplines.

Fearless Leadership
Managing Fear, Leading with Courage and Strengthening Authenticity
Morten Novrup Henriksen and Thomas Lundby

Clusters, Digital Transformation and Regional Development in Germany
Marta Götz

Gender Bias in Organisations
From the Arts to Individualised Coaching
Gillian Danby and Malgorzata Ciesielska

Entrepreneurship Development in India
Debasish Biswas and Chanchal Dey

Creating Business and Corporate Strategy
An Integrated Strategic System
Adyl Aliekperov

For more information about this series, please visit: www.routledge.com/Routledge-Focus-on-Business-and-Management/book-series/FBM

Creating Business and Corporate Strategy
An Integrated Strategic System

Adyl Aliekperov

Routledge
Taylor & Francis Group

NEW YORK AND LONDON

First published 2021
by Routledge
605 Third Avenue, New York, NY 10158

and by Routledge
2 Park Square, Milton Park, Abingdon, Oxon OX14 4RN

Routledge is an imprint of the Taylor & Francis Group, an informa business

Library of Congress Cataloging-in-Publication Data
Names: Aliekperov, Adyl, author.
Title: Creating business and corporate strategy :
an integrated strategic system / Adyl Aliekperov.
Description: 1 Edition. | New York : Routledge, 2021. |
Series: Routledge focus on business and management |
Includes bibliographical references and index.
Identifiers: LCCN 2021004599 | ISBN 9781032000619 (hardback) |
ISBN 9781032000633 (paperback) | ISBN 9781003172567 (ebook)
Subjects: LCSH: Strategic planning. | Business planning.
Classification: LCC HD30.28 .A375 2021 | DDC 658.4/012–dc23
LC record available at https://lccn.loc.gov/2021004599

ISBN: 978-1-032-00061-9 (hbk)
ISBN: 978-1-032-00063-3 (pbk)
ISBN: 978-1-003-17256-7 (ebk)

Typeset in Times New Roman
by Newgen Publishing UK

Contents

Figures

Tables

To the Readers

Here you can see the book is primarily aimed at suggesting the necessary repertoire of knowledge and skills for strategy creation with the help of the TASGRAM integrated system – Thinking, Analyzing, Strategy, Goals, Risks, Actions, and Monitoring. The advantage of the system is that it is rather structured, clear, and easy to use. Learning each stage of the TASGRAM system progressively, step-by-step, you will get a unique possibility to see the strategy being created on the example of Apple, Inc. In conclusion, the main outcome of the process will be presented – the strategy of Apple, Inc. created with the application of the TASGRAM system. You will see what a strategy looks like, where the boundary line is between a strategic and an operational levels of decision-making, and how these levels are interconnected.

Besides, you will find the answers to the following questions: What is strategy? Why is a competitor-oriented strategy no longer in the mainstream? What is the stakeholders' influence on the company's strategy?

The practical usefulness of acknowledged and reliable tools, such as PESTEL, VRIO, Stakeholder matrix, and others will be demonstrated. It will be discussed how they help in strategy creation, structuring, and directing the thoughts.

It should be emphasized that the book is addressed to rather a broad audience. Business school and university students will receive a unique chance to understand what strategy is, with the help of the author's arguments, theoretical research of Michael Porter and other well-known scholars and researchers, the examples of companies such as Apple, Inc., Amazon.com, Whirlpool, and so on. The process of how Apple, Inc. and Amazon.com, with the help of their strategies, are creating economic value, necessary for the development of the company, will be demonstrated.

Academic audience will be presented a new unique material for research and the chance to create the educational course "Strategy", based on the TASGRAM system. Through the application of TASGRAM system, it is very easy to demonstrate how a strategy is created, how strategic tools and frameworks interact with each other.

Practitioners, with the aid of the TASGRAM system, will get a convenient and understandable approach to the formation of the company's strategy. Those having doubts in the need for strategy will see global companies achieve impressive financial results on the basis of their strategies.

The book is written in a comprehensible and understandable manner; it contains many interesting facts and statistics. The author hopes that it will become a real assistant for creating a successful and effective winning strategy.

Sincerely yours,
Adyl Aliekperov, MBA

1 Introduction

"*Amat victoria curam*" is one of the best known ancient Roman phrases that is translated as "*victory loves concern*" (Enenkel et al., 2017:442). This phrase can be applied to companies and businesses that strive to take leading market positions. To assure their victory and to get thoroughly prepared for it, the companies create their unique strategies.

For instance, the strategy of General Electric (2019) is to provide constant and stable development, to improve their financial positions, and to strengthen their business. In order to accomplish this the company promotes its brand, improves its customer connections and attaches close attention to financial management. Besides, General Electric advances its "*lean management tools with a relentless focus on customer value*" (General Electric, 2019:2).

In Whirpool, the attention is focused on the idea that their "*long-term value creation strategy*" must improve their financial results (Whirpool, 2019:24). With this aim the company continuously develops its technologies and robotics, as well as offer its clients "*products that provide exceptional performance and desirable features*" (Whirpool, 2019:4).

The key strategy of Apple, Inc. (2019) are the future growth and the strengthening of marketing competitive position by investing in research and development, as well as in the development of new products and services and the renovation of the existing ones.

The example of these three leading companies showed that strategy determines the ways of its further development, prepares its coming victory, which is expressed in continuous growth and the creation of economic value.

This approach is also shared in academic literature. According to McKeown (2012:21), "*Strategy is about shaping the future*". Grant and Jordan (2016) operate the notion of "*successful strategy*", which includes the shaping of long-term goals, understanding the competitive environment, and the objective assessment of current resources.

Therefore, a single conclusion can be made that business needs a strategy that determines the direction of its functioning and further development. Moreover, Porter (2015) emphasizes that if a company deals with several multifaceted businesses, each of them needs its own strategy. Consequently, the issue of strategy creation and realization is a key factor that must be cared with the closest possible attention.

However, the following questions arise: what is strategy? how should it be created? and how should its realization be provided? It is the answers to these questions that this work is devoted to.

2   What Is Strategy?

This chapter, using the examples of companies such as Apple, Inc. and Amazon.com, and also the relevant theoretical postulates, suggests the answer to the questions "what is strategy?" and what is the difference between "business strategy" and "corporate strategy". Besides, the emphasis will be made on the advantages of customer requirements' orientation while creating the company strategy.

In 1996, Michael Porter asked the famous question "*What is strategy?*" (Porter, 1996). In 2000, professor of Strategy and Entrepreneurship Costas Markides remarked that "*we simply do not know what strategy is or how to develop a good one*" (Todorovich and Bakir, 2016). In 2015, Porter notes again that "*Strategy is relatively misunderstood in lot of organizations*" (Porter, 2015). In 2017, the opinion was voiced that many organizations do not completely understand what strategy is, mixing it up with planning (Latham, 2017). Hence, the question "*what is strategy?*" still remains topical.

Alongside this, Porter emphasizes that "*the essence of strategy is choosing to perform activity differently than rivals do*" and this idea must find its reflection in its unique market positioning (Porter, 2015).

Besides, according to Porter, a company must define the way it forms value proposition for its customers by means of its products or services (Porter, 2015). Weinstein and Ellison (2012) underline that value is not simply provision of services, quality image, and attractive price on a product or service, but also extraordinary efforts aimed at meeting or outrating a customer's expectations.

Thus, strategy is formed in terms of two aspects:

- Determining the company's market positioning aimed at its distinction in a competitive range.

- Determining the approach to customer value formation with the purpose of complete satisfaction or outrating the customers' expectations.

Consequently, strategy creation is concentrated on two stakeholders, that is, the company's customers and competitors. Concerning competitors, the company needs to specify its unique market positioning that makes it special in a competitive range. For its customers the company should shape a unique value proposition on the basis of marketing positioning.

What this looks like in practice can be illustrated with the examples of two companies – Apple, Inc. and Amazon.com. This gives an idea of the process of customer value creation on the basis of market positioning in the companies whose leadership and exclusive financial results are beyond doubt. These companies are included into "The Top 10" leadership list of companies, according to Fortune 500: Amazon. com takes the second place in this list and Apple, Inc. is given the fourth position (Fortune, 2020).

Apple, Inc.

On June 29, 2007 the smartphone iPhone was introduced to the world, which was a mobile telephone of an absolutely new format (Encyclopedia Britannica, 2019). The users obtained a unique possibility to thumb through the photos, made with the same smartphone, with a light finger touch to the screen, to exercise comfortable trips via the Internet, to perform other actions by means of a light contact with a touchscreen.

Besides, alongside with an innovative smartphone customers were offered the following innovative services (Fisk et al., 2014; Merchant, 2017; Straubhaar and La Rose, 2015):

- The website suggesting the information on the product, the ways of obtaining it and receiving support;
- Retail stores allowing potential customer to get to know more information about the iPhone and other company products;
- iTunes, a music shop where the iPhone owner could load music and listen to it;
- App Store, the Internet shop for applications to be installed into the iPhone;
- iCloud, the cloud storage, where reserve information copies placed on the iPhone and iPad can be stored. This service, in Apple's opinion, was one of the most meaningful variants, suggested by the

company. The customers got the opportunity of making a reserve copy of all their data and then to transfer them easily onto a new iPhone.

Not all services were suggested by the company simultaneously. Nevertheless, the customers could see that the company probably cares about their convenience, continuously suggesting new decisions that add value to its products and make them ever more attractive.

iPhone owners became attributed to a special group of people who possess this unique "made by Apple" gadget. It is noted that iPhone possession allowed people to demonstrate *"the shiny new thing, the one that everyone's talking about"* (Matyszczyk, 2018). A strong emotional and psychological link appeared between the company's brand and its customers (Lewis, 2014). It is worth saying that customers, who are emotionally linked with the brand, are ready to buy more products or services of this trademark, are more loyal towards price growth, often recommend this brand to other people, and communicate with the company willingly (Zorfas and Leemon, 2016). Besides, Apple, Inc. suggested the opportunity of creating one's own image: people could choose the most suitable accessories to protect their smartphones, empathizing by this their distinctness.

Steve Jobs emphasized that *"you've to start with the customer experience and work back to the technology"* (Hansen, 2013). In all appearances, this approach was realized in the iPhone creation, when customers' requirements were anticipated with the help of innovative technologies. The customers received a beautiful-looking, comfortable, and original innovative gadget that was a surprise for them. It was remarked that one of the secrets of the Apple smartphones' success was that the company managed to unite a gorgeous design with innovative approach.

Thus, it is possible to derive from the example of iPhone, the company's top-of-the-line product, that the company formed its customer value proposition by means of its product and the suggested services.

Weinstein and Alison (2012) note that the more attractive the value proposition is, which the company manages to form for its customers, the greater is the likelihood of achieving a high financial index. This statement was confirmed by Apple, Inc.

Owing to a well-made customer value proposition, the company really managed to take a leading market position, demonstrating its high financial results (Figure 2.1).

Such financial progress was managed by Apple, Inc. owing to the application of the differentiation strategy for the iPhone, singling it

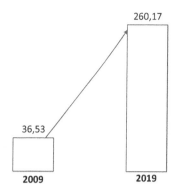

Figure 2.1 Annual total net sales of Apple, Inc. in 2009 and 2019
(in mln. USD).
Source: Apple, Inc. (2009, 2019, b).

out in the competitive range by means of unique products and services. It is necessary to note that differentiation is possible with factors such as technological progress and exceptional image, or when the relevant product possesses priority for the customers, and as a result, the company gets a considerable benefit compared to competitors (Porter, 1998). It was that Apple, Inc. demonstrated by its products and services. The company was guided by the fact that its products must be unique; owing to its revolutionary iPhone, it confidently sped up the flywheel of technological and image leadership, having created rather a valuable proposition for its customers.

The iPhone differentiation strategy also stated a high value-based price that enabled to generate a considerable profit. It is noted that the value-based prices are grounded on the product's unique characteristics (Dholakia, 2016). According to Nielson (2014), Apple, Inc. attempts to increase market demand for its products through differentiation, which entails making its products unique and attractive to customers.

Besides, the customers demonstrate a high loyalty and attachment level toward the Apple brand (Interbrand, 2019a). The main factors that have influenced the consumers' evaluation, owing to which Apple, Inc. took the first place among the 100 best-known brands, are the high level of exclusiveness of all Apple products and the "*differentiated proposition*" (Interbrand, 2019a).

So, the Apple, Inc. strategy looks like this:

1 **Marketing positioning:** the innovative company that considers the customers' requirements (strategy of differentiation).
2 **Creation of customer value:** unique innovative products and services plus an attractive image of the brand.

In Apple, Inc. they remark that the company believes it offers superior innovation and integration of the entire solution, including hardware, software, and services (Apple, Inc., 2019b). It is necessary to emphasize that this strategy is used by the company not only in relation to the iPhone, but for all its products and services.

For further realization of the chosen strategy, Apple, Inc. (2019b) is planning the following activities:

• To continuously develop and present innovative new products, services, and technologies to the marketplace;
• To exercise investments and pay close attention to R&D (research and development);
• To effectively stimulate the customers' requirements as to new and renovated products and services;
• To alter the concept of some stores *"to promote brand awareness"*
• To exercise continuous investments into the development of all company's stores;
• To continuously develop and improve "Digital Content Stores and Streaming Services".

In sum, all of the company's actions, its goals, and resources are aimed at maintaining and development of the sense of the chosen differentiation strategy – continuous innovative and technical development, creation of unique products, providing the necessary economic value, and allowing Apple, Inc. to distinguish itself in a competitive range.

Amazon.com

One of Amazon's most significant competitive advantages is a great amount of goods and services that are implemented on its online platform Amazon.com. (Aliekperov, 2021). This can be explained by the fact that 58% of all goods and services on the Amazon.com platform are offered by third-party sellers (Amazon, 2018). The rest, like Kindle electronic book, is presented directly by Amazon. Owing to such approach, the customers of Amazon.com have constant access to a wide varieties of goods and services, consisting of 67 groups, which include hand-made products and health goods (Amazon Services, no data). To all goods and services, especially to those of "Alcohol" and "Baby Products" groups, Amazon.com makes strict demands as to their quality and safety (Amazon Services, no data).

It is underlined that the quality of goods or services is one of the main requirements of the customer and is also the basic requirement of any person (Stevenson, 2015; Maslow, 1970).

Special attention is given to the electronic platform Amazon.com. As it was shown by the conducted analysis of Amazon.com, the platform has a friendly user interface, necessary instructions, and a feedback form. The customers receive unique personalized propositions based on their purchases and preferences. Bezos states that Amazon is "*working to build a place where customers can find and discover anything they want to buy, anytime, anywhere*" (Bezos, 1999:3).

It should be noted that Amazon.com strives to beat its customers' expectations. For instance, the company is "*working toward offering One-Day Delivery*" instead of two-day delivery, announced earlier, for the Prime service subscribers (Amazon, 2019b).

Bezos underlines that "*the company intends to build out a significant distribution infrastructure to meet all customers' demands in the best way*" (1998:3).

Thus, Amazon formed its own unique approach of creating the customer value:

1   The variety of goods and services meeting certain criteria.
2   Convenient and affordable service for their purchase.
3   Communication with the customers.
4   Personalized customer propositions.
5   Maximally prompt delivery.

This proposition rests on two key strategies: cost leadership and differentiation. The cost leadership strategy presumes the obtaining of competitive advantage by proposing the customers the most attractive prices (Porter, 1998). The strategy of differentiation, as already stated, is a technological progress, an exceptional image, or the priority of presenting corresponding goods to the customers; as a result the company gets a considerable profit compared to its competitors (Porter, 1998).

Amazon.com (no data, a) states that the company "*consistently works toward maintaining competitive prices on everything we carry*". In his letter to shareholders of 1997, which is attached to each new letter to shareholders, Bezos (1997) notes that Amazon's priority will always be the creation of customer value and the maintaining of the most attractive prices on products and services.

For instance, as soon as the government of the UK announced about its plans to *"stop charging VAT on online publications because of the pandemic"* related to COVID-19, Amazon instantly confirmed that *"it will cut the price of its Kindle ebooks"* (Waterson, 2020). For the subscribers of the Prime service, the company continuously guarantees *"Amazon's low price, with fast free delivery and much more"* (Amazon.com, no data, b). According to independent estimates, Amazon.com is the *"overall industry price leader"* (Profitero, 2018).

Bezos (letters 1997–2018) emphasizes that Amazon will always differ from other companies by its outstanding customer centricity and innovativeness. For instance, Amazon.com achieved a considerable progress *"using AI in its retail business, has pioneered voice recognition technology (Alexa) and platform-based services (Amazon Web Services)"* (Boston Consulting Group, 2019).

The research data of the Boston Consulting Group showed that in 2019 Amazon took the second place among the most innovative global companies (Boston Consulting Group, 2019). Besides, Amazon took the third place among 100 companies in the level of the customers' trust and loyalty (Interbrand, 2019b).

The respondents gave a special mark to Amazon's ability to effectively satisfy the customers' requirements, to its positive image, and the ability of continuous development (Interbrand, 2019b).

Bezos underlines that *"we're proud of the differentiation we've built through constant innovation and relentless focus on customer experience"* (1998).

Thus, Amazon's strategy can be characterized in the following ways:

1 **Marketing positioning:** innovative and customer-centered company (strategy of differentiation) with acceptable price policy (strategy of cost leadership).
2 **Creation of customer value:** the variety of quality goods and services, and convenient innovative services as to their purchase and shipment.

The essence of Amazon's strategy, with the help of which it differentiates itself in the competitive range, is innovative decisions, customer centricity, attractive prices, various goods, and convenient services.

The company maintains the development of its strategy by means of the following initiatives:

• Continuous development of customer centricity level, based on the analysis of the customers' requirements: it is critical to ask customers what they want, listen carefully to their answers, and figure out a plan to provide it thoughtfully and quickly (Bezos, 2018).

- Innovative approach: in Amazon the closest attention is given to *"machine learning and artificial intelligence, Internet of Things, and serverless computing"* (Bezos, 2017).
- Attractive price policy: in 2017 Amazon suggested its customers a new version of hands-free speaker with voice control – Echo *"with an improved design, better sound, and a lower price"* (Bezos, 2017).

The chosen strategy enabled Amazon.com in achieving unbelievable financial results (Figure 2.2).

It is possible to observe from the cases of Apple, Inc. and Amazon. com that following the strategy helped these companies to achieve a convincing growth, financial success, and economic value. It is this that can be characterized as the main strategic goal – the company's financial well-being. Owing to financial success only will the companies be able to invest in the development of society, provide their personal development, and invest in further sustainable development.

Business strategy is the approach under which companies determine the present ways of creating customer value and form a unique positioning as against their competitors with the purpose of creating economic value. According to Porter (2015), business strategy is *"a core strategy"* for company.

However, Porter (2015) emphasizes that if a company is going to diversify its business and to expand it, it must create its "corporate

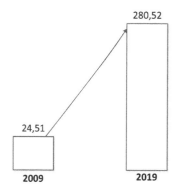

Figure 2.2 Annual total net sales of Amazon.com in 2009 and 2019 (in mln. USD).

Source: Amazon.com (2009, 2019, a).

strategy". According to Pidun (2019) the corporate strategy defines the future development of the company.

It is probably in this point that the answer to the question is hidden, why many leaders and managers find it difficult to understand *"what is strategy"*. Evidently, here a simple confusion is observed between a business strategy and a corporate strategy. So, a distinct differentiation of a business strategy and a corporate strategy is necessary:

- Business strategy is the company's positioning and the creation of a customer value at the present time.
- Corporate strategy defines the future development of the company. Within the framework of a corporative strategy a company will be able to deal with the following issues: diversification, integration, and purchasing of new businesses.

In this chapter the emphasis will be made on the analysis of both business and corporate strategies. What are the ways of cooperation between a business strategy and a corporate strategy, how they influence one another will be demonstrated in Chapter 3.

Schematically a company's strategy can be presented as shown in Figure 2.3. The suggested diagram is a convincing demonstration of the fact that the company's goals and its strategies are not the same thing. Porter (2015) emphasizes that without determining a strategy, a company will find it difficult to signify the goals providing its development, and only clarity in strategy leads to clear goals.

It should be noted that the company's products or services must fully correspond to its market positioning in which the approach to forming customer value is denoted. In other words, if a company positions itself as an innovative one, it should be reflected in its products or its service. In case if the company does not correspond to the plot of its market positioning, the company may lose its customers' trust, which will doubtlessly have a negative influence on its financial success. For instance, a company's product contains no innovative layouts; however, the company is positioned on the market as an innovative one. Consumer Policy Research Centre (2017) notes that trust is the basis of customer–company cooperation. In case of discrepancy between market positioning and value proposition, the customers will gradually stop paying attention to the company's products, which will have a negative influence on its financial indices. There may be another situation: a company makes really innovative products, but this has no reflection at all on its marketing positioning. In this case the company will experience a financial loss because of incorrect marketing positioning, which

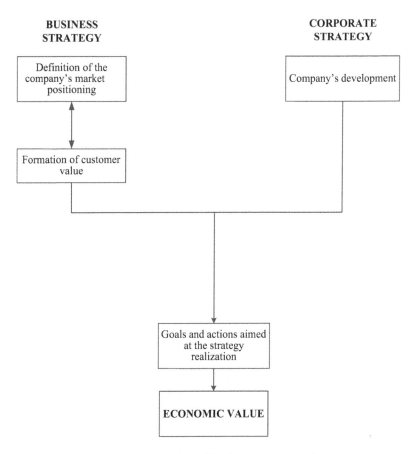

Figure 2.3 Schematic representation of business strategy and corporate strategy.

does not provide the customers the information on the advantages of the product.

For instance, Amazon.com simultaneously exercises market positioning both based on strategy of differentiation and on cost leadership. Hence, the company must maintain and extend its innovativeness level and continuously pay attention to technologies allowing the offer of competitive prices. Innovations, new technologies, and acceptable price policy will help Amazon.com continuously develop its market positioning and generate economic value.

Apple, Inc. following the strategy of differentiation for its products must also pay attention to continuous innovative improvement, that is, by offering new innovative products to the market. Only in such a way the company will be able to create an expected customer value and confirm the strategy of differentiation, based on its products' specialness. Porter (1998) emphasizes that a company, which proposes a unique product, can always expect the customers' loyalty to prices on its products or services, which are somewhat higher than those of its competitors.

It is important to focus again on the fact that market positioning is not simply a declaration of intentions, but an approach that makes the basis for creating customer value.

It should be noted that Porter (1998) calls his vision of strategy creation "Competitive strategy", making the main accent on "*Techniques for Analyzing Industries and Competitors*". He also notes that "*competitive strategy, and its core disciplines of industry analysis, competitor analysis, and strategic positioning, are now an accepted part of management practice*" (1998:IX). He indeed underlined that "strategic position" also "*can be based on customers' needs*" (1996). However, the following fact is quite remarkable: in Porter's (1998) book *Competitive Strategy*, there are only about 229 words associated with "customer" (customer, customers, customization, etc.), and about 1518 words associated with "competitor" (competitive, competitors, competitor, competition, etc.). Later he more clearly emphasizes the fact that strategy is "*how to deliver unique value to the customers we try to serve*" (2015).

However, the fact remains that for today there exists a universally recognized "Competitive strategy" by Michel Porter (1998), in which the main accent is laid on the necessity to distinguish a company in a competitive range. But, it is the customers and not competitors who pay money for the products and services suggested by companies. "*Obsess Over Customers*" – here is one of the most famous Jeff Bezos' (1997) quotations. And here also Amazon.com is not alone. Lead Director of General Electric (GE) remarks "*putting customer first*" (General Electric, 2020:1). This phrase is supported by real actions. For instance, the company implements the lean management system for the best satisfaction of the customers' requirements (General Electric, 2020). Besides, GE created specialized "Customer Experience Centers", where cooperation and communication with the customers on a wide range of questions take place (General Electric, 2017).

Global clothing and sports goods manufacturer Adidas declared that "*we are consumer-focused*" Adidas (2012:3). Walmart, Inc., which has the top position in the Fortune-500 list, emphasize *"we earn the trust of our customers every day by providing a broad assortment of quality merchandise and services at everyday low prices"* (Walmart, Inc., 2020; Fortune, 2020).

Samsung that takes a lead in the production of consumer electronics and smartphones has affirmed that *"customer satisfaction constitutes one of the most important fundamental factors in securing a company's competitive edge"* Samsung (2017:50).

Thus, today's reality requires the shift of accents, that is, focusing more on customers, but not on competitors. Consequently, business will regularly need "customer-centered strategy", the sense of which is in line with the customers' requirements. It is necessary to observe that this approach absolutely does not mean the absence of company's attention for its competitors, as competition among companies has not been cancelled. But they compete with each other to acquire a greater number of customers first of all. So, strategy is first of all about customers, but not about competitors.

Chapter 3 discusses the following two questions: how to combine customer centricity with attention to competitors? and how to shape a strategy and denote all necessary actions for its realization? As an example for customer-centered strategy creation, the company Apple, Inc. and its main product iPhone, which forms approximately 55% of the company's net sales, will be chosen. It is stated that Apple's success is the success of its main product iPhone, in the first instance (Aten, 2019).

3 TASGRAM – The Integrated System of Strategy Creation

This chapter presents the system of strategy creation – TASGRAM. With the example of Apple, Inc. it will be clearly demonstrated how the use of this system helps to create the business and corporate strategies.

The system of strategy creation – TASGRAM – consists of seven constituents:

1 Thinking
2 Analyzing
3 Strategy
4 Goals
5 Risks
6 Actions
7 Monitoring

Veber (1964) stated that all tasks must be divided into functions, which will allow to obtain a more effective result. It is this approach that is applied in the TASGRAM system, in which each constituent, with the help of the corresponding tools, performs its unique task, facilitating the creation of the company' strategy. The details of the TASGRAM system are presented in Table 3.1.

In addition, each constituent of the strategy-creating TASGRAM system and its applied tools will be described in detail. Taking Apple, Inc. as an example, it will be clearly demonstrated how the successive application of the system's constituents and of its corresponding tools will enable the business strategy and the corporate strategy creation.

As the applied tools are cross-industrial, the obtained knowledge will help in further application of the TASGRAM system to create the strategy for any company.

Table 3.1 Description of the TASGRAM system constituents

Constituent	Task	Tools and frameworks
Thinking	Determination of the company's preliminary business strategy for its further analysis and final approval.	Strategic thinking scheme.
Analyzing	Collection and analysis of information necessary for taking strategic decisions.	**Analysis of industry:** - PESTEL - Five FORCES
		Analysis of a company: - VRIO analysis
		Stakeholder analysis: - Stakeholder matrix - 5W Client analysis
		Product portfolio analysis: - BSG matrix
Strategy	On the basis of the information obtained, the final business strategy is created and the corporate strategy, determining the further development, is worked out.	- Porter generic strategies - Ansoff matrix
Goals	Formulation and expert report of the goals the achievement of which facilitates the business strategy and corporate strategy realization.	- Goals' evaluation on the basis of SMART analysis - Joint table of goals
Risks	Determination of risks influencing the strategy realization	- Risks identification, analysis, assessment and reaction. - Joint table of risks
Actions	Determination of actions aimed at the achievement of the goals facilitating the business strategy and corporate strategy realization.	- Joint table of actions
Monitoring	Determination of indicators to control the realization and effectiveness of the business strategy and corporate strategy.	- Joint table of indicators
Finalization	**Strategic table of the company**	

At the end of this chapter, a strategic table is suggested, which in a generalized form will reflect the main sections of the strategy of Apple, Inc. created with the help of the TASGRAM system.

Constituent 1: Thinking

There certainly exist many various approaches for the creation of strategy, defining necessary actions aimed at its achievement. However, strategy creation should begin with a simple and understandable process – "Thinking". Baldoni (2012:125) notes that "*sound purpose begins with sound thinking-with taking time to think before we do*".

In this case it is necessary to think over the company's future strategy or to reinterpret the already existing one. Betz (2016:vii) remarks that "*strategic thinking is about imaging a future world and taking a sequence of short term actions to achieve it*". According to Olson and Simerson (2015), strategic thinking is grounded on finding answers to the questions about the main topic of reflection that must be achieved, and what the main problems will have to face.

Jack Welch emphasized that "*strategy is a living, breathing, totally dynamic game*", and it is necessary to "*ponder less and do more*" (Welch and Welch 2005:165, 166). Undoubtedly, in the dynamic world of today's business there is no time for thinking or meditation. But very often, because of the "*pressure for results*" people are obliged to act too fast, which at times makes them "*take a step back and make thinking a priority*" (Baldoni, 2012). Hence it is extremely important for the future success to begin the creation or reinterpretation of the strategy from thinking. However, the process should not be very long and must be maximally concentrated.

According to Wootton and Horne (2003), strategic thinking can be exercised according to the following scheme shown in Figure 3.1.

It should be reminded that strategy is the creation of customer value, which is determined on the basis of market positioning. Consequently, the first object for thinking must be the customers – their satisfaction with the company's value proposition and its market positioning. There is a direct dependence between the successful customer cooperation, definition, and consideration as to the customers' requirements on the one hand, and gaining of the necessary profit on the other hand (Aliekperov, 2021).

Then it is necessary to think about a product or service. On this basis the company creates a unique customer proposition and generates economic value, necessary for further development. It is logical: before promising anything to the customer, the company must be sure that

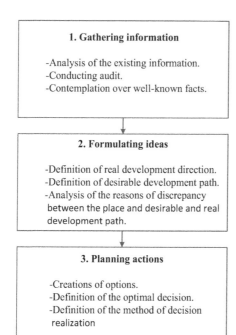

Figure 3.1 Strategic thinking scheme.

its products or services completely corresponds to the value that the customers are going to receive after purchasing it.

And finally, by means of contemplation it is necessary to find the answer to the question if the business strategy allows generating economic value.

It is worth noting that at this stage only a preliminary hypothesis for further analysis and adopting the existing strategy or correcting it for developing alternatives is being worked out. In other words, this stage is a kind of a trigger for the final strategy formation. At this stage, as well as at all the following stages, the business strategy, defined in Chapter 2 of this book, will be analyzed: the Apple, Inc. business strategy, with the accent on its basic product – the iPhone – that generates about 55% of the company's net sales (Apple, Inc., 2019):

1 **Market positioning:** the innovative company that considers the customers' requirements (strategy of differentiation).

2 **Creation of customer value:** unique innovative products and services plus an attractive image of the brand.

So, thinking starts with an analysis of Amazon.com' customers satisfaction. According to the Interbrand (2019) data, the brand "Apple" takes the first place in the level of customer loyalty. Furthermore, the most meaningful company's characteristics, marked by its customers, are the following (Interbrand, 2019a):

1 The possibility to identify oneself with the brand;
2 The brand's unique characteristics and differentiation;
3 The brand's accordance to the customers' value proposition.

Besides, Apple, Inc. (2019) demonstrates rather a confident dynamics of total net sales amounting to 260,174,000,000 USD in 2019.

Thus, high total net sales, with forms due to customers' activity, shows that customers are active in purchasing the company's product/service despite the fact that Apple, Inc. establishes premium prices on its smartphones. For instance, as one can see on Apple's (no data, d) site, the price of iPhone 11 Pro starts at 999 USD. The cost of Galaxy S10 on the site of Samsung Company (no data, a) starts with 749 USD. According to expert assessment, these smartphone models have approximately similar characteristics (McGarry, 2020). High net sales demonstrate that premium price establishment on smartphones is a winning strategy for Apple, Inc.

Therefore, the company's business strategy on the basis of differentiation and with consideration to the creation of value proposition, embracing the following facts can be called successful:

• The company receives a considerable economic value, enabling its active development.
• The customers express high appreciation because the fact that the company's products stand out from the similar competitive range, which provides a meaningful sense of iPhone's exclusiveness, as well as of the rest of the products.
• The customers identify themselves with the brand.

However, there also exists a negative tendency, demonstrated by the company's flagship product – the iPhone. In 2019, as compared to 2018, the iPhone demonstrated net sales decline by 14%, which influenced the total net sales to decline by 2% (Apple, Inc., 2019). Other products and the services demonstrated a positive growth.

Further on, the analysis showed the lowering tendency of the Apple's share in Premium Smartphone Segment Market Share: it was 58% in 2017, 51% in 2018, and as to the first quarter of 2019 it was 47% (Mishra, 2019; Pathak, 2019a).

Alongside this, against the same period, the shares of Apple's competitors on Premium Smartphone Segment Market Share grew: Samsung had 23% in 2017 and 25% in 2019 (Q1), Huawei had 8% in 2017 and 16% as to the first quarter of 2019 (Mishra, 2019; Pathak, 2019b). This data, of iPhone losing its market share, is also affirmed by expert evaluations (Fingas, 2019; Browne, 2019).

Besides, Apple, Inc. started losing its technological leadership, duplicating the achievements of other smartphone manufacturers. In 2009, HTC Company brings on the market a smartphone with 4.3-inches display picture size (Fingas, 2013). In 2011, Samsung offered its customers Galaxy Note with 5.3-inches display picture size (Samsung, 2015). And only Apple, Inc. persistently made smartphones with 3.5-inches display picture size, presenting a new iPhone with a 4-inch display picture size only in 2012 (Williams, 2019).

In 2018, Samsung introduced its first smartphone with a triple-camera setup (Carman, 2018). At the same time, Apple was only preparing for the introduction of a new iPhone 11 with a triple camera (Gartenberg, 2019).

Gad (2016:3) emphasizes that if "*the brand had previously given their customers reason to anticipate spurring innovations*" and does not meet expectations, the customers start losing trust for the brand. It is stated that Apple's success is the success of its main product iPhone, in the first instance (Aten, 2019). Thus, if iPhone stops generating the necessary customer value, it can have a negative impact on the success of the whole company.

Alongside this, the company's CEO Tim Cook states that "*Apple innovates like no other company on earth ...*" (Apple, 2019, c). However, facts suggest that there appears a discrepancy between the real and the desirable position of the company. For example, Apple.com increased the size of the iPhone screen much later than its competitors.

Two fundamental principles of the Apple, Inc. strategy – innovativeness and exceeding customer satisfaction, which constitute the basis of the company's strategy – stopped playing their strategic role.

Because innovations are a key issue of a business strategy and its customer value proposition, the company should maintain its strategy with real innovative solutions that make the products unique and desirable for the customers.

The summarized conclusion of the "thinking" stage is as follows:

- Apple's differentiation strategy and the creation of customer value proposition on its basis is still a trump-card for the company. The customers express their trust for the brand and the company's products, which has a positive reflection on financial results, despite some downswing of net sales.
- For the full-fledged realization of the chosen strategy, the company should enlarge its investments into research and development, with the purpose of raising the innovativeness level of the iPhone, as it is the main profit generator.
- It is necessary to pay more attention to customer relations, analyze the customers' preferences, and substantiate them in the company's products and services. It is essential to remember that the first iPhone's success consisted in the fact that the company had exceeded the customers' expectations.

This conclusion was drawn on the analysis of information on Apple's rating concerning the trust for this brand, net sales analysis, and possible reasons of iPhone net sales decline. In other words, the audit of the current information was conducted based on the recommendations of the strategic-thinking scheme (Figure 3.1), contemplations about the known facts. As a result, a discrepancy was noted between the declared approach and the implemented one, and then the solution for the discovered problem was suggested.

In sum, after the preliminary approval of advisability following the existing strategy, it is necessary to pass to the next stage – to "Analyzing". At this stage, the information will be collected for the final statement, the correction of the existing strategy or the creation of a new one, and also for determining the goals and the action for their realization.

Constituent 2: Analyzing

It is worth noting that no company exists in vacuum. Porter (2014) remarks that *"strategy is a big picture of how organization is going to win in its environment"*.

According to Porter (2014), each company has its own *"inherent attractiveness for a point of view of profitability"* and certain industry where it competes. That is why, to take a final decision as to its strategy, it is necessary to exercise the analysis of the industry where the company operates. The main aim of industry analysis is to determine external factors influencing the effectiveness of the company's business, as well as the attractiveness of the industry itself (Grant and Jordan, 2016). Besides, it is necessary to conduct the company analysis with the purpose of defining its unique advantages owing to which it enters into competition on the market and create value for customers. Moreover, the company's strategy is also influenced by its external and internal stakeholders, such as the personnel, suppliers, employees, shareholders, and so on. Freeman and McVea emphasize that managers need to understand the concerns of shareholders, employees, customers, suppliers, lenders, and society, in order to develop objectives that stakeholders would support (Freeman and McVea, 2001). Therefore, besides the industry and company analyses, attention will also be given to the stakeholder analysis, for determining the key stakeholders, influencing the realization of strategy. The key place in this analysis must be given to the No.1 stakeholder, that is, to the company's customers. Kotler and Keller (2016) note that the customer is the company's main stakeholder and the level of interrelations with him or her determines the company's successful development. Drucker (2008:98) points out that *"There is only one valid definition of business purpose: to create a customer"*. As it was already pointed out, global leading companies, such as Adidas, General Electric, Samsung, and others, give strategic attention to their customers and their requirements, which again proves that the stakeholders must be paid the closest attention.

Besides, at this stage Apple's products and services portfolio will be analyzed. The main purpose is the formation of optimal portfolio, which would present certain value for the customers and provide the company with economic value and the necessary growth.

Thus, the stage "Analyzing" consists of four kinds of analysis:

1 **Industry analysis.** Tools applied: PESTEL and Porter Five Forces
2 **Company analysis.** Tools applied: VRIO Analysis
3 **Stakeholder analysis, with the focus on the main stakeholder – the customers.** Tools applied: Stakeholder matrix and 5W Client Analysis
4 **Company portfolio analysis.** Tools applied: BCG Matrix

Zanoni (2012) notes that strategic analysis is the collection, elaboration, and assessment of data necessary for taking strategic decisions. Further on, a detailed approach for conducting each analysis and the tools applied will be discussed.

Industry Analysis

For conducting the industry analysis, two tools are applied: PESTEL and Porter Five Forces of competition frameworks.

PESTEL

PESTEL analysis is the broad macro-environment of organizations in terms of political, economic, social, technological, environmental, and legal factors (Johnson et al., 2008). It allows to determine key drivers influencing the future development of the industry (Johnson et al., 2008). Besides, the analysis defines the trends, determining the development of the industry. In the given case, the industry of smartphone production will be analyzed, in which Apple, Inc.'s key product – the iPhone – is the competitor. As it was noted, this is the main Apple, Inc.'s product generating profit.

So, the purpose of conducting the PESTEL analysis is to denote the drivers that will exercise their impact on the development of smartphone industry, and the existing trends.

Conducting the PESTEL analysis is discussed in the following:

POLITICS

Constant impact of political factors on the smartphone industry.

Supporting Rationale

- China--US trade wars (Reuters, 2020b)
- Apple fined a record $1.2 billion by French antitrust authorities (Amaro, 2020)
- US sanctions against HUAWEI (Bershidsky, 2019)

Conclusion: Apple, Inc. should exercise the monitoring of legislations, analyze political activity in the countries where it operates, with the purpose of exclusion of negative effects on the business.

ECONOMICS

Impact of the pandemic caused by the COVID-19 virus on the smartphone industry and the population's incomes.

Supporting Rationale

Negative Factors
- According to Gartner (2020) research, global smartphone sales declined by 20% in first quarter of 2020 due to COVID-19 impact.
- Apple closed its stores because of the COVID-related pandemic (Apple, no data, c).

- In 2020, global smartphone shipments in February sank from 99.2 to 61.8 mil. units, if compared to February 2019 (O'Dea, 2020).

Positive Factors
- The greatest economies of the USA and Germany begin restoring after pandemic (Rattner and Miller, 2020; Reuters, 2020a).
- Active measures are being taken to rehabilitate the EU economy (Strupczewski, 2020).
- Stabilization of export-oriented Chinese economy is expected in the nearest time (He, 2020).
- As shown in the Apple's condensed consolidated statements of operations (six months ended, unaudited) of 2020, the company's total net sales in March 2020 are somewhat higher than in March 2019 and the growth constituted about 5% (Apple, Inc., 2020). This index was formed due to the sale of the service, while the products' sale somewhat dropped.

Besides, attention should also be paid to population's incomes. According to the Apple's (2019) annual report, the main trio customers of its products are from the following regions:

- America
- Europe
- Greater China

On the back of the World Bank data (no data), between 1990 and 2019 these regions demonstrated stable GDP per capita growth (Table 3.2).

After the rehabilitation of the world economy, Apple, Inc. will evidently have a stable market for realization of its products again.

Conclusion: the data shows that despite the pandemic and the reduction of the smartphone sales, Apple, Inc. demonstrates a positive

Table 3.2 GDP per capita (in USD per annum)

Region	Date\GDP per capita	
	1990	*2019*
USA	23 888	65 280
China	317	10 261
European Union	14 794	46 467
Rest of the world	4 285	11 435

dynamics in the net sales. Besides, the hope for the fast restoration of world economy, the positive tendency as to GDP per capita in key regions and the rest of the world are prompting that the company will not fully sense the consequences of the pandemic-related crisis.

However, Apple, Inc. must carefully watch this process and its possible impact on the company, because the company's smartphones differ by their premium price. Consequently, if the people's incomes drop, it can have a negative effect on the customers' possibility to purchase the company's main flagship product – the iPhone.

The need in situation monitoring is caused by the absence of clear guarantees that the pandemic will not be repeated (Euronews, 2020).

In the event of a greater damping of demand for smartphones, because of a considerable population's income drop, the company will probably have to revise its model range by producing gadgets with a more affordable price. For instance, the price of the iPhone SE in 2016 was about 395 USD (Digg, 2018).

SOCIAL

The growth orientation on the customers' requirements: customer centricity.

Supporting Rationale

Today, companies are extremely aware of the fact that their main goal is to establish a constructive dialogue with the customers, to understand their individual requirements, and to offer them the required products and/or services (Kotler and Keller, 2016). This approach has formed the cornerstone of customer centricity (Fader and Toms, 2018). According to Pemberton (2018), customer centricity is the strategic priority for most companies and *"the new marketing battlefront"*. The customer centricity trend has a cross-industrial character. It is stressed in Huawei Company (2019) that "customer satisfaction" is one of the key elements the Board of Directors pays attention to. In Disney (2019) they are confident that their reputation fully *"depends on many factors including the quality of our offerings, maintenance of trust with our customers and our ability to successfully innovate"*. Hilton (2019), the famous hotel network, defines that *"The goal of each of our brands is to deliver exceptional customer experiences and superior operating performance"*.

Quite a serious factor, prompting companies to consider the "client voice", is the clients' requirements as to the products and services. For instance, the customers' requirements as to the smartphones' technical characteristics are growing progressively. In particular, this finds its expression in the following: they continuously focus their attention on the need to make the capacity of battery larger, to provide a *"high-resolution screen with excellent color reproduction"*, with an improved camera, better design, to provide a more comprehensive data store (Barnes, 2017).

Moreover, the customers will doubtlessly demonstrate their preference to the company that will not only meet their requirements, but will exceed them, proposing a product or service that will satisfy their requirements in the best way.

Berry (1995) emphasizes that the customers want the company to hear their voice and to consider individual requirements. It is such an approach that leads to establishing stable links between the company and the customers (Berry, 1995). Research proves that only long-term relations between a customer and a company, grounded on trust relationships, produce a positive influence on the company's financial results (Kumar, 1999). Apple's closest competitor, Samsung (2016), stressed that to build a trusting relationship with customers and partners is one of their top priorities.

Therefore, when the sense of the business is oriented toward a high level of customer centricity, on complete trust between the customers and the company, on continuous consideration and satisfaction of customers' requirements, and on effective customer communications, these enable the company to be financially successful and to possess the ability to confidently determine its future development.

Conclusion: Apple, Inc. should not only watch and realize the customers' requirements with more care, but anticipate these requirements with the help of newly innovative solutions. Besides, the company must build long-term customer relationships, as well as effective communications grounded on complete customers' trust for the company; in other words, the company must be more customer-centric.

TECHNOLOGICAL

Rapid technological change.

Supporting Rationale

- At present, active implementation of the 5G technology, *"the new cellular standard"*, is in progress (Chen, 2020). Consequently, even today companies should analyze the question: which is the next standard going to be and how it will influence the setup of smartphones.

- Elon Musk and Jeff Bezos are working simultaneously on two projects – "Starlink" and "Kuiper" (Sheetz, 2020).
- These projects should help people get high-speed satellite broadband Internet all over the globe. This will also probably require certain changes in smartphones' technology.
- Frequently, the technologies related to artificial intelligence are being used (Agomuoh, 2018).

Conclusion: Because of the fact that the customers' requirements as to continuous technological advancement of smartphones are growing, application and realization of new technologies will constitute the basis of customer centricity development, by proposing the customers more technically perfect and convenient products and services.

ENVIRONMENTAL

Attention to environmental matters.

Supporting Rationale

Carrol and Buchholtz (2009) stress that today's business and society are inextricably linked, and they influence one another's development not only by trade relations but also through other factors. One such aspects is the company's attitude toward environmental matters.

It is stated that people more willingly buy the product of the company that demonstrates its care for the environment and adherence to "green marketing" (Cone Communications, 2017). Green marketing can be defined as the effort by a company to design, promote, price, and distribute products in a manner that promotes environmental protection (Polonsky and Rosenberger, 2001).

At the moment, three leading smartphone producers – Apple, Inc., Samsung, and Huawei – pay closest possible attention to environmental protection.

Apple, Inc.   It is stated by the company that they achieved their aim and are *"covering 100 percent of our operations with 100 percent renewable electricity"* (Apple, 2019, a).

It has been especially emphasized by the company that they are continuously working toward lowering the energy consumption of their products, for instance, *"the 11-inch iPad Pro models are more than 69 percent more efficient than the ENERGY STAR standard"* (Apple, Inc., 2019).

The emphasis is made on the fact that *"historically, Apple's carbon footprint has paralleled its financial performance"* (Apple, Inc., 2019). In other words, the clear dependence between the carbon-footprint decrease and the growth of profit level is being traced in the company.

Samsung   The company states that *"Samsung is committed to minimizing the environmental impact of its innovative products, which include smartphones, TVs and much more"* (Samsung Newsroom, 2017). According to statistics presented by Samsung, *"86 percent of Samsung products in development had attained ratings of Good Eco-Product or higher"* (Samsung Newsroom, 2017).

Huawei   The Huawei (no data, a) Green World report runs that the company *"is committed to promoting green ICT solutions"*. Besides, the company has set a goal for itself: to drive industries to conserve energy and reduce emissions and build an environmentally friendly low-carbon society that saves resources (Huawei, no data, a).

Conclusion: Apple, Inc. must develop initiatives in the green marketing sphere, as it allows not only to increase the customers' loyalty for the brand, make its contribution to the improvement of the environment, but also to produce a positive influence on the finance indexation.

LEGAL

Consumer Privacy

Supporting Rationale   Fifty two percent of tech, media, and telecom respondents rank data privacy among top three policies most impactful to their business (PWC, 2020). This can be explained by the following two factors:

- More and more people use smartphone as the means for payment and storing personal data.
- Many countries exercise legal regulation of personal data security:
  - UK – The Data Protection Act 2018 (Gov.uk, no data).
  - EU – General Data Protection Regulation (Official Journal of the European Union, 2016).
  - Australian Privacy Act (Australian government, 2018).
  - In the USA, a document is in preparation, which regulates the sphere of personal data security; besides, on the level of separate states similar laws are already in operation (National Law Review, 2020; Curac-Dahl, 2019).

Conclusions: On account of focused attention to the problem of using smartphones as the storage of personal data, on the part of state regulatory bodies, Apple, Inc. must pay closest attention possible to the development of technologies that would allow guaranteeing the personal data security.

As a result of conducting PESTEL analysis, the following drivers and trends, preconditioning the industry's development, were determined:

Drivers

Customer centricity: maximum attention to the customers' requirements, which is expressed through effective communications in building long-term relations grounded on mutual trust between the customers and the company.

Innovations and technologies development: customer centricity must be based on continuous technological improvement, innovation of new products and services, and meeting or anticipating customers' needs.

Trends

The PESTEL analysis allowed bringing out the main trends influencing today's development of the smartphone industry:

* Constant impact of political factors
* Pandemic's influence on the customers' purchasing power
* Adherence to green marketing
* Personal data security

Porter Five Forces

Hereafter, the analysis of the industry where the company operates will be continued with the help of Porter's Five Forces tool. This tool enables one to understand the nature of competition in the industry where the company operates and in defining the necessary actions that facilitate strategy creation and realization. Besides, the industry attractiveness will be evaluated. Schematically, Porter's Five Forces can be represented as shown in Figure 3.2.

Detailed description of each factor (Porter, 1998, 2008; Grant and Jordan, 2016) is given in the following sections.

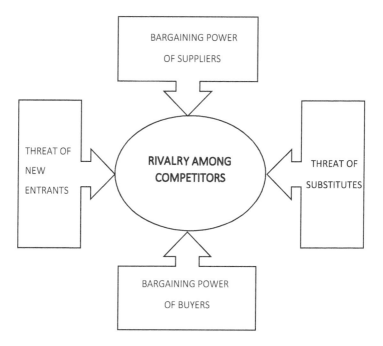

Figure 3.2 Porter's Five Forces.
Source: Porter, 1998, 2008; Grant and Jordan, 2016.

THREAT OF NEW ENTRANTS

If entry into the market and effective competition require not very much money and effort, or key technologies are badly protected, competitors can make a quick entry into the market and weaken the company's position.

Industry is attractive: it is difficult for potential competitors to enter into the company's market.

Industry is not attractive: it is easy for potential competitors to enter into the market.

BARGAINING POWER OF SUPPLIERS

This power is analyzed from the standpoint of how easy it is to find on the market the alternative to existing suppliers, in the event that the quality of supplier cooperation is unsatisfactory, or that the supplier increases the prices. Consequently, the more suppliers there are on the market, the easier it is to find the necessary alternative. And vice versa, if the number of the necessary suppliers is limited, it makes their position stronger as to their ability of dictating the conditions they need.

Industry is attractive: there are enough alternative suppliers present on the market.

Industry is not attractive: it is difficult for the company to find alternative for the current suppliers.

BARGAINING POWER OF BUYERS

The basis for the analysis is the following points: how easy it is for the company's customers to move to the competitors, whether the customers can influence the company's process and demand extended service. In addition, it is necessary to note that the fewer customers the company has, the more power they have to influence the company.

Industry is attractive: the customers find it difficult to transit from one company to another and to cooperate with another company.

Industry is not attractive: the customers have no difficulty as to the transition from one company to another and cooperating with another company.

THE THREAT OF SUBSTITUTES

Porter notes that "*A substitute performs the same or a similar function as an industry's product by a different means*" (Porter, 2008:14). For instance, services such as WhatsApp, Viber can serve as email substitutes, as they also allow sending text messages and attached files. More accessible products or a service-substitute can easily weaken the company's position, which will produce a negative effect on its profitability. As far as smartphones are concerned, the only probable substitute can be a smartphone produced by a competitive company.

Industry is attractive: it is problematic for the customers to find an alternative for the offered products or services.

Industry is not attractive: the customers can easily find an alternative for the offered products or services.

RIVALRY AMONG COMPETITORS

According to Porter, "*High rivalry limits the profitability of an industry*" (Porter, 2008:15). On the market with a big quantity of rival companies, customers will always be able to exercise a transition from one company to another for purchasing similar products or services.

Industry is attractive: there are not a great number of companies that are in the state of competitive rivalry.

Industry is not attractive: there are a great number of companies on the market that are in the state of competitive rivalry.

Each of the elements of this analysis is rated on the following scale: low, medium, and high.

Thus, with the help of Porter Five Forces, the nature of competition in the smartphone industry will be analyzed, as well as the influence of rival forces on Apple, Inc.

THREAT OF NEW ENTRANTS

The threat of new entrants to the market, capable of creating the competition to the iPhone, has no fundamental significance as of today. First of all, this finds its proof in two factors: high cost of creating a similar company and the need for investments in the brand development. According to statistical data, in the period between 2015 and Q4 2019 the trio of the smartphone market leaders remained unchanged: Samsung (17.3% market share Q4 2019), Apple, Inc. (17% market share Q4 2019), and Huawei (14.3% market share Q4 2019) (Gartner, 2016, 2020).

That's why it is possible to assume that the appearance of new entrants will present no threat for Apple, Inc. in the near future.

The power of new entrant: low.

THE POWER OF SUPPLIERS

It is stated in Apple, Inc. that *"most components essential to the Company's business are generally available from multiple sources"* (Apple, 2019:3, b). However, it is emphasized that *"the Company uses some custom components"*, which are not used by the competitors and which can be delivered only *"from only one source"* or *"limited sources"* (Apple, 2019:3, b).

The substantial fact is that Samsung, the nearest competitor, is the only company that can make OLED displays, NAND flash, and DRAM chip in the quantities that Apple, Inc. needs for its iPhones, which are the main revenue driver for Apple (Gartenberg, 2017). Thereat, Apple's relations with this supplier are far from very positive ones. For instance, in Q2 2019, Apple, Inc. paid nearly $684 mil. to Samsung because Apple, Inc. didn't meet the minimum order quantity (Adnan, 2019).

Attention should be paid to the fact that *"Company's hardware products are manufactured by outsourcing partners that are located primarily in Asia"* (Apple, 2019:3, b). For instance, Apple, Inc. keeps the noticeable part of iPhone production in China (Reisenger, 2019). Barboza, (no data) emphasizes that about half of all iPhones now are made in a huge manufacturing facility in the central Chinese city of Zhengzhou. As the PESTEL analysis showed, the political factor has rather a considerable impact on the industry, and the risk of trade wars between the USA and China still remains. Experts note that the Apple, Inc. depends on Chinese sales and labor and the company has become a focal point in the trade war (Reisenger, 2018).

In an attempt to lessen its dependence from China, Apple, Inc. also considers the diversification of its industrial capacities and their partial transition to such countries as India, Vietnam, and Indonesia (Snouwaert, 2020; GSM Arena, 2020).

Thuswise, Apple, Inc. depends to a great extent on its suppliers providing the delivery of unique components and on the manufacturers of its products situated in the third countries.

The power of suppliers: high.

BARGAINING POWER OF BUYERS

Apple, Inc. takes the first place in the level of customers' loyalty for the brand (Interbrand, 2019a). Besides, the company demonstrates rather high net sales that are formed owing to buying activity. Though, the fall in net sales of their flagship product, the iPhone, therewith is rather high and constitutes 14%. Likewise slowly the percentage of people using the iOS operation system is falling too, and the number of Android users is growing (O'Dea, 2020). This fact shows that the customers, despite their demonstration of brand loyalty, started looking for options other than the company's products.

Hence, the power of the customers can be estimated as a medium one, as they still confidently buy the company's products, demonstrating their trust for the brand. Apple, Inc. should pay more attention to the analysis of the clients' requirements, for innovative solutions and technological improvement of the products and service.

The power of buyers: medium.

THE THREAT OF SUBSTITUTES

The iPhone's substitute can be not only a device having similar characteristics and quality, but also possessing the same aura of attractiveness that the Apple brand and its products are famous for. Therewith, it should be stated that Samsung, according to Interbrand (2019, b), has the sixth place in the level of customers' loyalty and only five positions away from Apple's first place. The weighty characteristic is the authenticity of the Samsung brand, its ability to create the needed customer value. One of the most probable alternatives for the iPhone, according to experts, is Samsung Galaxy S20 Ultra (Kidman and Jager, 2020).

Thuswise, Apple, Inc. has a very strong competitor on the market represented by the products of Samsung. However, Samsung has not yet reached Apple's level as to the customers' embracement of the brand. Besides, Apple, Inc. has rather a considerable competitive advantage presented by the service ecosystem, supporting the company's products (Cipriani, 2019). It is noted that *"Apple's ecosystem is key to its success"* (Haselton, 2017).

In this case, Apple, Inc. also should pay attention to innovative and technological development of its products and services for better satisfaction or anticipation of the customers' requirements. Only in such a way the company will be able to retain its market leadership.

The threat of substitutes: medium.

RIVALRY AMONG EXISTING COMPETITORS

According to the data of Q4 2019, two leading smartphone manufacturers – Samsung (17.3%) and Apple (17.1%) – take approximately equable market shares, and Huawei, with its 14.3%, rounds out as the top three leaders (Gartner, 2020). At the same time, about eight famous smartphone manufacturers, except Apple and Samsung, are present on the market (Technavio, 2019).

These facts indicate that the competition in the industry is rather intensive. If Apple, Inc. does not support its strategy with real innovative projects, with analysis and realization of the customers' requirements, this power has all the chances of transforming itself into a real threat for company and first of all, for its flagship product – the iPhone. In this situation when the development of the industry is determined by customer centricity, the companies should focus their efforts on the creation of the best value proposition for the customers that would meet or anticipate their requirements.

The threat of rivalry: high.

Overall conclusion: despite the fact that in the industry, high competition and the high power of suppliers are observed, there exists the danger of substitute appearance, nevertheless the company's exit from this industry is not considered by absolutely any means, because of Apple's strong competitive positions – the strong brand name, unique products, and loyal customers.

It should be pointed out again that to retain its leadership positions Apple, Inc. should pay its closest attention to continuous technological improvement and innovativeness of its products and services.

Company Analysis

Having received the idea of the smartphone industry, it is necessary to analyze which characteristics distinguish Apple, Inc. in its competitive range and how the company will continue to generate the customer value. For this, the application of VRIO analysis is suggested. The main aim of the VRIO analysis is to estimate the situation inside the company, to define its unique resources and capabilities that make it competitive on the market (Peng, 2009). The analysis is based on the following characteristics:

- **V** – is it valuable? – to which extent this option is interesting for the customers or the company?
- **R** – is it a rarity? – how unique is this option compared to similar options, products, or services?
- **I** – is it imitable? – how difficult it is to imitate this option?
- **O** – organizational – how optimal it is exploited by the organization?

If each of the points under evaluation receives a "yes" (X) answer, this option can be considered as a sustainable competitive advantage. If it receives two or three "yes" answers, then this is a temporary competitive advantage for a short period and is not sustainable. If the option receives four "no" answers then this is a competitive disadvantage.

On the basis of the exercised analyses of the industry and the information derived from the first "thinking" stage, for conducting analysis with the use of the VRIO frameworks, the application of the following resources and capabilities that allow the company to generate client value and successfully compete on the market are expected (Table 3.3)

Table 3.3 VRIO analysis

Apple's Organizational Resources & Capabilities	V	R	I	O
Products	X	X	X	X
Service ecosystem	X	X	X	X
Brand	X	X	X	X
Global distribution network	X			X

- Company's products
- Company's service ecosystem
- Brand
- Global distribution network

Company's Products

As of today, the company offers customers its main product, the iPhone and Mac with iPad. Besides, Apple, Inc. offers customers the products from the category "Wearables, Home and Accessories", to which belong the Apple Watch, Air Pods, and the Home Pod Smart Speaker (Wolverton, 2019). Simultaneously, Apple, Inc. suggests the most harmonious cooperation between the service, "hardware" and "software" (Apple, Inc., no data, a; Moren, 2020). Choosing various iPhone models, the users can be fully confident of the fact that the software will be equally convenient and familiar by experience. Quite meaningful is the fact that Apple is always just-in-time about upgrading the software, up to the latest version (Costello, 2020; Hill 2020).

It is also necessary to note that, besides the smartphone Samsung Galaxy S20, experts named the smartphone OnePlus 7T as the best alternative for iPhone 11. However, the detailed comparative analysis of the two smartphones enabled reaching the final verdict: "Overall winner: iPhone 11" (Ismail, 2019).

Thus, the company's products and generating rather big net sales, iPhone in particular, and also being supported by the brand power are the basis for Apple's unique value proposition for its customers. They are sought-after by the customers and are at the top value for the company. However, if the company does not pay enough attention to the technical upgrading of its products or to the development of new innovative products, this competitive advantage will be lost.

Brand

According to the "Best Global Brands 2019 Rankings", the cost of the Apple brand constitutes USD 234.241 mln. (Interbrand, 2019a). In this customers' loyalty and trust for the brand rating Apple, Inc. takes the first place, while its closest rival in the smartphone market Samsung has the sixth place with the brand's cost of USD 61.098 mln. (Interbrand 2019). It is stated that a brand with a significant level of customer loyalty attracts customers more than a comparable brand with a less customer loyalty (Schneiders, 2011). Owing to its products, the "Think differently" slogan Apple, Inc. managed to create a really unique brand (Johanson and Carlson, 2015).

The Company's Service Ecosystem

Apple, Inc. possesses a unique ecosystem for its products' support, and a website, suggesting information on the products, iTunes – music store, iCloud – the cloud storage, AppStore – the store for software applications, the service for online payments – Apple Pay and many others.

On the market there are, certainly, enough alternative variants. For instance, Google Pay is the alternative for Apple Pay. The service, similar to AppStore, is also offered by Google for Android telephones. Samsung (no data, b) also offers the similar service for its smartphones – Galaxy store. There also exists an adequate proposition of services-analogues in iTunes (Agarwal 2020).

However, the company managed to achieve a high degree of integration between their services and devices, because it is only Apple, Inc. that fully controls the hardware and software in its products (Cipriani, 2019). This fact doubtlessly upgrades the security and comfort level as to the use of the Apple service. It is stated that the service, suggested by Apple, added exclusive value to the company's products, and consequently, it exercises the most positive influence on the customer experience (Moorman, 2012).

Thuswise, at the moment the service support given to Apple's products can be rightfully considered to be a unique and valuable company resource, which represents the value of the highest degree for the customers and a difficulty for the competitors at the creation of an analogous ecosystem.

Global Distribution and Sales Network

The products of Apple, Inc. can be bought across the globe by means of the Apple online store and distributers, retail stores, which provided potential customers the possibility of independently knowing the iPhone and other company's products (Apple. com, no data, b, e). The closest Apple's competitors – Samsung and Huawei – keep to the same scheme (Samsung, no data; Huawei, no data, b).

The Apple brand and the unique design allow the company to successfully distinguish their stores in the competition range. And still, this approach is rather widely spread and is successfully copied by the competitors.

Key conclusions: The company's products, its service ecosystem, and especially the brand constitute the sustainable competitive advantage of Apple. It is noted that owing to the company's brand reputation and its unique products, the company can set premium prices on its products (Morgan and Houston, 2019). These options must be continuously developed, as they constitute the basis for customer value creation. Besides, the company should invest in the development of the marketing network for the selling of products and services, and differentiate it from the similar competitors' networks.

Stakeholder Analysis

Freeman (2010) observes that under the "rough-air" conditions it becomes more evident that the opinion of the stakeholders in creating and implementing a strategy must necessarily be considered, and their participation in the process of the strategy realization must be provided. To stakeholders they refer *"all parties who will be affected by or will affect strategy"* (Bryson, 2004). Berry (1995) emphasizes that the company defines its most important stakeholders itself.

Therewith, according to Freeman (2016), the following stakeholders are most important for an organization:

- **Suppliers**, who strive to make the business better by supplying quality products or services.
- **Employees**, who provide the creation of a product/service, with the help of which the company creates customer value.
- **Communities**, in case their wishes as to the company's activity are neglected, restrictive measures can be introduced which hinder the conducting of business.

In addition, Freeman (2016) distinguishes customers among the most important stakeholders. Kotler and Keller (2016) emphasize the exceptional role of this stakeholder in a company's development. This is clearly explained by the fact that customers' activity completely determines such a top-important company indicator as net sales.

The interests of owners, investors, shareholders must be considered too (Freeman, 2016; Carrol and Buchholtz, 2009). This stakeholder can restrict the company's activity in the event that they disagree with its strategy, or if the value proposition, which first of all is associated in this group with the profit, is absent (Carrol and Buchholtz, 2009).

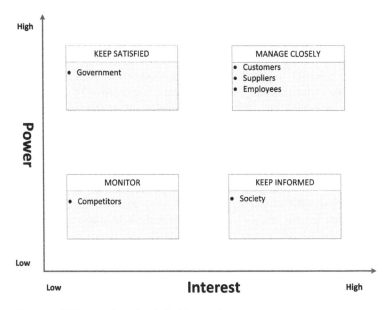

Figure 3.3 The results of stakeholder analysis.

The given matrix enables identifying the stakeholders which directly or indirectly influence the organization strategy (Mendelow, 1981) (see Figure 3.3).

Suppliers

According to the information resulting from the Porter Five Forces analysis, suppliers have rather a high power, as concerns Apple, Inc. It is observed that certain components are currently obtained from single or limited sources. Besides, the key condition of Apple's operation is the closest cooperation with enterprises which manufacture the company's products, and are located in Taiwan, have branch offices in China and other countries: Foxconn, Wistron, Pegatron, Compal (Moorhead, 2019).

Consequently, the relationships with these stakeholders must be top-productive and must be continuously monitored by the company.

Conclusion: impact on the company – strong. Close cooperation is necessary.

Employees

Norton and Kaplan (2005) state that it is necessary to *"align employees' competency development plans, and their personal goals and incentives, with strategic objectives"*.

This can be explained by the fact that it is employees who in the end are responsible for the strategy's key element – the creation of customer value. It is also noted that *"Effective communication to employees about strategy, targets, and initiatives is vital if employees are to contribute to the strategy"* (Norton and Kaplan, 2005).

Consequently, Apple, Inc. must continuously get the personnel engaged into the strategy's creation and realization, communicate to the employees the main goals of the company. Norton and Kaplan (2001:210) observes that strategy must be *"everyone's everyday job"*.

Conclusion: Impact on the company – strong. Close cooperation is necessary.

Communities

One of the aspects the customers may pay attention to is the company's attitude to ecology. According to Kotler and Keller (2016), people more willingly buy the product of the company demonstrating its care for society and for the environment. The data of PESTEL demonstrated that Apple, Inc. follows green marketing principles, paying immediate attention to nature protection issues. It is pointed out by the company that this produces the most positive influence on its financial results.

Apple's attention is also paid to the issue related to a person's and society's basic requirement – to safety. It is safety which is the basic requirement of any person, as Maslow (1970) observes. In Apple, Inc. significant resources to network and data security are distinguished. Demonstrating socially responsible behavior, Cook, CEO of Apple Company, emphasizes that *"We care about the user experience. And we're not going to traffic in your personal life. I think it's an evasion of privacy. I think it's – privacy to us is a human right"* (Ghaffary, 2018).

The company sends an explicit signal to the society that cooperation with it is absolutely safe, as the company care about the society and ecology.

Thus, Apple, Inc. must continuously develop socially important initiatives, informing the society and local communities about it.

Conclusion: Impact on the company is not expressed very distinctly. It is necessary to regularly inform the society on socially meaningful initiatives.

Government

According to the PESTEL data, one of the trends influencing the development of the smartphone industry is the current political factor. Consequently, Apple, Inc. must give its closest attention to the legislation of the countries where the company's products are present; some other activity is exercised, with the purpose of prevention of political or economic sanctions related to the company. Stakeholders possess considerable power to influence Apple's operation.

Conclusion: Impact on Apple, Inc. rather essential. It is necessary to trace that the company activity is exercised according to legislative requirements.

Competitors

The Five Forces analysis showed that the closest competitors constitute quite a meaningful power in the struggle for the leading position on the smartphone market.

However, they have no real power over Apple, Inc. and can shatter the company's positions only by creating a more valuable proposition for the customers, having applied more innovative methods in manufacturing of their products. So, the company must carefully monitor their activities and use all efforts to be a leader in realization and creation of new innovative products and services.

Conclusion: Impact on the company is inessential. Exercising active monitoring of the competitors' activity is necessary.

Shareholders

According to Carrol and Buchholtz (2009), shareholders constitute a serious power that can influence the company's activity and proceeding from this fact, the closest cooperation and interaction must be organized with them. Apple, Inc. pays the closest attention to cooperation with this stakeholder, which finds its expression in press releases and other information about financial performance, information on corporate governance, and details related to the Company's annual meeting of shareholders.

Conclusion: A high rate of impact on the company. Close cooperation is necessary.

Customers

Concluding the stakeholder analysis, a detailed customer analysis will be exercised, as they are the main stakeholders influencing one of the most important indicators of the success of the company's work, of its strategy – net sales. This indicator shows the income obtained by the company within a definite period from the sale of goods or services to the company's customers (Tracy, 2002). Thus, a customer is the key stakeholder of the company, who produces a direct impact on its ability of generating economic value.

The company's activity must be aimed at the following: customers are meant not only to buy the company's services or products, but they must become the company's long standing partner, making repeated purchases. Consequently, the company needs the knowledge of the customers' preferences, of what they expect from the cooperation with the company, with the purpose of creation of the best value proposition. For this, the 5W Model of Customers' Analysis is suggested (Ferrell and Hartline, 2008).

This analysis answers the following questions:

1. WHO ARE POTENTIAL CUSTOMERS OF THE COMPANY?

Statistical characteristics of the company's potential customers are considered:

- Demographical features (gender, age, income)
- Geographical features (continents, countries, etc.)
- Psychographic characteristics (habits, interests)

2. WHAT CUSTOMERS DO WITH A PRODUCT?

Which characteristics of the product/service are used by the customers and, consequently, add value to the product. Being aware of the specifics of the customers' use of the products, the company will be able to invest into the development of these or those characteristics, thus aiming at the fullest satisfaction or anticipation of the customers' requirements.

3. WHERE DO CUSTOMERS PURCHASE PRODUCT?

This enables the best understanding of the way the customers make purchases, of where it is most convenient for them to do it. For instance, online or in physical stores. Consequently, the company will be able to suggest the customers the most convenient channels of purchasing the products/services.

4. WHY DO THE CUSTOMERS CHOOSE A DEFINITE PRODUCT? WHAT ATTRACTS
THEM THE MOST?

The answer to this question will help the companies to most effectively
exercise the market positioning of the product, to improve the most
important features, specific for the products or services.

5. WHY WON'T THE CUSTOMER BUY THE OFFERED PRODUCT? WHAT WILL MAKE
HIM REFUSE FROM IT?

The companies will be able to understand which actions or their absence
will negatively effect the customer's wish to purchase the product or
service.

5W Model of Client Analysis

1. Who? – statistical characteristics of the iPhone customers

- The iPhone users can be provisionally nominated for up to 65 years
  old (Lehrer, 2020).
  - The iPhone is preferred mostly by female customers, 51% are
    female customers and 49% are male customers (Hixon, 2014).
    However, the difference is inessential.
  - According to statistical data, the number of iPhone users in the
    world is distributed in the following way (in mln.): USA – 120,
    China – 228, rest of the world – 380 (O'Dea, 2020).
  - It is stated that having an iPhone or an iPad is more likely an indi-
    cator of its owner's high income (Salisbury, 2018).
  - iPhone users are rather educated people: 27% are university
    graduates or have PhD degrees, 38% have college education or
    higher (Hixon, 2014; Statista, 2013).

For instance, the customers' denotation of their profession allows
offering mobile apps typical of a particular professional activity. If the
company wants to enlarge the number of its male customers, it is necessary to analyze more carefully their demands to smartphones and try
and realize them.

2. What customers do with a product?

According to the survey of 2000 smartphone users in Great Britain,
27% stated that they hardly used their telephones for calls during a week

or more (Express, 2017).Besides, according to respondents' answers, the following most frequently used smartphone possibilities were selected:

1. Texting (88% use this)
2. Email (70%)
3. Facebook (62%)
4. Camera (61%)
5. Reading news (58%)
6. Online shopping (56%)
7. Checking the weather (54%)
8. WhatsApp (51%)
9. Banking (45%)
10. Watching videos on YouTube (42%)

Thus, the survey showed that the great majority of the user's activities are related to the work in the Internet. It is noted that 61% used their smartphone as a camera. Judging from this information, the users need a convenient use of the Internet on their smartphones, convenient apps, and a display with optimal size. It is also necessary to pay attention to upgrading the camera's possibilities as to exercising quality video and photo shoot, which will lead to the expansion of the cloud space, the telephone memory for the storage of photos and personal documents. A special attention must be given to data security, as 45% of customers answered that they used their smartphones for bank transactions. The provision of safety against the users' e-mail correspondence hacking is also necessary. As the PESTEL showed, security is the today's trend determining the development of the smartphone industry.

3. Where do customers purchase product?

As can be seen in the site of Apple Company, an iPhone can be purchased in the Company's online stores and in Apple Stores (Apple, Inc., no data, e). Besides, an iPhone can be purchased from distributors (Apple, Inc., no data, b). Consequently, the customers' buying activity must be the subject of continuous watching, and investments should be made into the most popular ways of purchasing of Apple's products/services.

4. Why do the customers choose a definite product? What attracts them the most?

• Apple suggests a unique ecosystem that interacts with its devices and adds them a considerable value: "iTunes, the App Store iOS, macOS, Apple TV, Siri and Home all tie together". Once a consumer invests in the ecosystem, it is harder to switch out of it (Haselton, 2017).

- User friendly software interface iOS (Elgan, 2011).
- Generally, the iPhone is very convenient and *"Phone remains the easiest phone to* use" (Spoonauer, 2019).
- *"Apple doesn't release its source code to app developers, and the owners of iPhones and iPads can't modify the code on their phones themselves"* (Norton, no data). That is why the Apple's devices and the iPhone are prevented from data leak and hacking (Norton, no data).
- iPhone allows its owners to emphasize their statuses. According to Bailey et al. (2019:33), iPhone contains the *"strongest status signal".*

This list cannot, apparently, be called an exhaustive one, but evidently the main reasons explaining the people's wish to purchase the iPhone were presented. On the whole, the respondents who changed their telephones to Android on the iPhone noted better user experience as one of the main reasons for this change (Power, 2017).

Thus, the main reasons for purchasing an iPhone are as follows:

- A unique service system
- Convenient use
- Personal data security
- The smartphone's attractive image

So, Apple, Inc. have to invest into the development of these options.

5. Why won't the customer buy the offered product? What will make him refuse from it?

If we judge from the factors that drive customers to purchase the iPhone, their absence will have an adverse effect on the customers' wishes. For instance, if the iPhone stops being convenient for use or its unique ecosystem will change for the worse, this will not be a motive for choosing the iPhone.

Besides, one of the characteristics which has driven the respondents to choose the Apple brand as the most attractive one is its uniqueness, its ability to distinguish itself in a competitive range (Interbrand, no data, a).

Consequently, if the customers see that the brand is no longer unique and does not generate the necessary value, they will demonstrate lesser willingness to buy iPhones and other company's products.

Experts also point out that present-day iPhones have no distinguishable exquisite design (Spence, 2019). Because of this factor too, the customers will not, probably, favor Apple's smartphones as their choice.

Conclusion: Based on this analysis the company should hear the "customers' voice" and define their requirements. By combining the data of this analysis with the information of the industry analysis on the fact that the customers demand continuous technical upgrading of the product, innovative solutions, it is possible to formulate a real value proposition, coming ahead of the competitors. It is necessary to underline, that customer is a key stakeholder of Apple, Inc. and close cooperation is necessary.

In sum, the Stakeholder analysis enabled distinguishing the most important company's stakeholders and determining the level of cooperation with them.

Product

And finally, the concluding stage of this section is the analysis of Apple's products and portfolio with the help of the BCG matrix that analyses products and business "*by market share*" and "*market growth*" (Sutherland and Canwell, 2008). The main aim of this analysis is the shaping of optimal products/services portfolio that could provide the company's necessary growth (Pruschkowski, 2015). Owing to the company's service or products the company competes on the market and creates a unique proposition for its customers (Aliekperov, 2021).

This matrix consists of four squares:

Dogs: these are products having a low market share and a low market growth. These products do not provide big profits, but they do not require great investments either.

Cash Cows: enjoy the customers' popularity. They have a high market share, but not the highest demand, that is why too great investments should be avoided.

Stars: these are the products with a high market share and a high market growth, so they are on the way to advance.

Question Marks: these products have no considerable market share and do not provide a high profit. Nevertheless, they can turn up "Stars" or "Cash Cows" if given slightly bigger investments.

According to the Apple Form 10-K of 2019, the company's net sales were formed for an account of the following products and services (Apple, Inc., 2019):

1. iPhone
2. Mac
3. iPad
4. Wearables, Home and Accessories
5. Services

iPhone: Between 2016 and 2019 the number of smartphone users in the world grew from 2 500 000 000 to 3 500 000 000, and the estimates for 2021 is 3 800 000 000 bill. (Bankmycell, no data).

Thereat, it is necessary to note that the net sales positive dynamic is observed as to iPhone: in 2014 the figure was USD 101.991 mln. (Apple, 2016). In 2019 this index grew by USD 40.39 mln. and constituted USD 142.381 mln. (Apple, 2019, b). Considering these facts and also the fact that among all Apple's products the iPhone exercises the greatest influence on the net sales, this product must be attributed to the "Star" category and its development must be invested into, despite the fact that in the period between 2018 and 2019 certain lowering of this product's net sales was observed.

Mac: The share of households with a computer at home grew worldwide from 27.3% in 2005 to 49.7% in 2019 (Alsop, 2020). Besides, some positive dynamics is demonstrated by Mac net sales, from USD 24.079 mln. in 2014 to USD 25.740 mln. in 2019 (Apple, Inc., 2014, 2019). The data shows that the demand for this product will remain, and it can also be attributed as a "Star" product.

iPad: According to the statistical data, the share of similar products on the global market dropped from 3.76% in June 2019 to 2.81% in June 2020 (Stat counter, 2020). Similar period in the USA market demonstrated the following lowering dynamics: from 7.7% to 4.5% (Stat counter, 2020). Besides, in the period between 2014 and 2019 in Apple, Inc. (2014, 2019), this product's net sales dropped from USD 30.283 mil. to USD 21.280 mil. However, between 2018 and 2019 a positive tendency as to iPad net sales from USD 18.380 mil. to USD 21.280 mil. is observed (Apple, Inc., 2019). Nevertheless, the negative trend, including the market share lowering, can be clearly seen.

Thus, the product can be attributed to the "Dogs" category. Despite its low market share, it still provides considerable net sales for the company. Great investments in this product's development are evidently not advisable, and the company should produce it while the demand remains. Probably, one of the factors of the lowering demand for this product is the fact that smartphones are substitutes for iPads.

Service: As the VRIO analysis showed, the company's unique service ecosystem is Apple's competitive advantage. According to the customers' analysis, the service ecosystem is one of the main factors facilitating the customers' choice of Apple's products. At the same time, the service demonstrates rather an optimistic dynamics of sales (USD 46.291 mln. in 2019) with a 16% growth compared to the previous year (Apple, Inc., 2019).

Consequently, the service should be attributed to a "Star" category, the investments into its development should be continued as it is quite an important addition that enhances the competitive fitness of the Apple's products and demonstrates a confident-enough dynamics of sales.

Wearables, Home and Accessories (Apple Watch, HomePod, Apple TV, AirPod): These products demonstrate rather a confident upward dynamics in the period from 2017 (12.826 bill.) to 2019 (24.482 bill.) (Apple, Inc., 2019). It is remarked that *"Apple's Wearables and Hearables business has become a very big part of Apple's continued growth strategy"* (Reisinger, 2019). Wearables, Home and Accessories should be attributed to "Stars" category.

Analysis showed that Apple's portfolio mostly consists of products and services of the "Stars" category, which can perfectly maintain the strategy of further growth and generate economic value necessary for the company (Figure 3.4). However, taking into consideration the fact

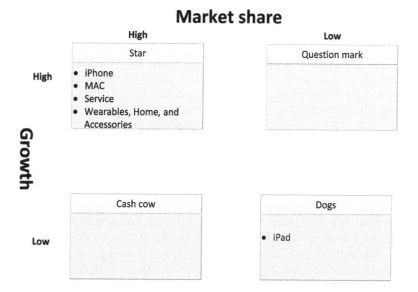

Figure 3.4 BCG matrix. Results of the analysis conducted with the BCG matrix.

that today the company has only one flagship product that generates 55% of its net sales and demonstrates certain lowering of sales, the company should exercise the analysis of its opportunity of product range extension. It is noted that consumers expect the next product to be the next big thing – and when it isn't, they don't hide their disappointment (Lee, no data).

So, the analysis of Apple Company portfolio is the concluding stage of "Analyzing" chapter. However, before passing to the next stage, it is necessary to sum up all the obtained information as shown in Table 3.4. The structured and clearly presented information will be further used for the strategy creation, for defining the goals, for risks evaluation, and for determining the necessary actions and monitoring their success.

Table 3.4 Joint table ("Analyzing")

ANALYZING

Industry analysis

Drivers:
- customer centricity;
- innovations and technologies development.

Trends:
- adherence to green marketing;
- personal data security;
- the influence of the pandemic on economic activity, the threat of natural calamities;
- the influence of political factors.

Power of new entrant: low. In the nearest time Apple, Inc. should not be on guard against new competitors.
The power of suppliers: high. The company depends on the suppliers of some components, and also on third companies, manufacturing Apple's products.
Bargaining power of buyers: medium. Customers confidently purchase the company's products, demonstrate their trust for the brand, however there exists the drop of net sales of the main company's product, the iPhone, which is a negative factor.
Threat of substitutes: medium. Apple, Inc. has a strong market rival represented by Samsung. However, Samsung still concedes to Apple, Inc. in the level of trust and customers' loyalty for the brand and, consequently, for the products.
Rivalry among existing competitors: high. Apple's nearest competitor, Samsung, takes approximately the same market share as Apple does. Simultaneously, about 10 competing manufacturers are present on the market.
On the whole, the industry cannot be characterized as an attractive one, however, Apple, Inc. is the leader and has rather serious competitive advantages; so leaving this industry is unreasonable.

(*continued*)

Table 3.4 Cont.

ANALYZING

Company

The company's main competitive advantages are:
- Brand
- Product
- Service ecosystem
- In a somewhat smaller degree – the products' sales network

Stakeholder analysis

- **Suppliers, employees, shareholders, government:** the closest cooperation.
- **Customers:** the closest cooperation, full meeting and anticipation of this stakeholder's requirements.
- **Society:** continuous information provision is necessary as to the company's contribution in the society development and environmental programs.
- **Competitors:** continuous monitoring of the competitors' market activity.

Portfolio analysis

The company has a well-balanced portfolio, which enables suggesting value necessary for the customers and generating economic value required by the company. However, today Apple, Inc. has only one flagship product (iPhone) which generates 55% of its net sales and demonstrates some drop of sales, so the company should analyze its possibility of extending its product range.

Constituent 3: Strategy

At this stage it is necessary to analyze once more the pre-denoted strategy of Apple, Inc. for its approval, correction, or for adoption of a new strategy. It will be shown how the information of the sections "Thinking" and "Analyzing" is used for the final creation of business strategy of Apple, Inc., and for determining the corporate strategy.

So, the pre-denoted Apple's business strategy looks in such a way:

1. **Market positioning:** the innovative company that considers the customers' requirements (strategy of differentiation).
2. **Creation of customer value:** unique innovative products and services plus an attractive image of the brand.

Analyzing the viability choice of the stated strategy for its final approval or change can be exercised with the help of the Porter Generic Strategies analysis (Porter, 1998).

The sense of this analysis lies in determining the company's market positioning by means of the suggested options: focus strategy, cost leadership strategy, differentiation strategy.

Focus Strategy

Companies that use focus strategy concentrate on definite niche markets. Understanding the dynamics of this market and their customers' unique requirements, the companies develop inexpensive or unique for this market products. The application of focus strategy in target niches presupposes the choice of cost strategy or differentiation strategy.

Advisability of the strategy application: according to the information obtained from the analysis of 5W Customer, about 750 mln. people throughout the world use iPhones. Consequently, the application of focus strategy at the moment is not advisable for consideration.

Cost Leadership Strategy

Allows receiving competitive advantage at the cost of the most attractive price.

This goal within the Cost leadership strategy can be achieved owing to:

- Profit growth at the cost of reduction in expenditure and simultaneous price reduction.
- Market share growth at the cost of lower prices.

Companies that manage successful leadership in prices share usually have:

- Access to assets necessary for investments in technologies that will lead to the reduction in expenditure.
- Effective logistics.
- Low cost of baseline expenditures.
- Policy of stable prime cost reduction.

The greatest risk for this strategy realization is that the sources of expenditure reduction will be copied by the competitors that is why it is important to constantly find the ways for cutting the costs down.

Advisability of the strategy application: the information of the section "Thinking" showed that the existing business strategy was attractive for the customers. It allowed the company to generate high net sales, establishing premium prices on its flagship product.

Consequently, the application of cost leadership strategy is not advisable for consideration.

Differentiation Strategy

The strategy presupposes that products or services suggested by the company are more attractive than those of the competitors. This attractiveness depends on the specifics of the industry character and the product; it can be determined by functionality, durability, service support, and brand image.

To achieve success in differentiation strategy company must demonstrate:

- Innovations and the significant technical improvements.
- The possibility to deliver high-quality products or services.
- Effective sales and marketing, demonstrating the advantages suggested by the differential proposal.

If companies stop following these conditions they will run the risk of losing their competitive advantage.

Advisability of the strategy application: According to the information from the VRIO analysis, Apple, Inc. has necessary resources for following the differentiation strategy:

- A competitive unique product that constitutes customer value.
- A unique service ecosystem supporting the company's products.
- A unique brand, which, owing to the company's products, confidently highlights the company in its competitive range and creates additional customer value.
- Necessary infrastructure for the products' realization.

Thus, the requirements corresponding to the differentiation strategy are observed:

- The possibility to deliver high-quality products or services.
- Effective sales and marketing, demonstrating the advantages suggested by the differential proposal.
- A unique brand.

As a consequence, Apple, Inc. can set premium prices facilitating the creation of the necessary economic value; and this is demonstrated by the company.

However, differentiation strategy also presumes research, innovations, and constant technological improvements. As the section "Thinking" demonstrated, in relation to its flagship product iPhone that generates 55% of net sales, Apple, Inc. does not demonstrate innovativeness of an adequate level. Considering the PESTEL data on the issue that the development of the smartphone industry is determined by continuous technological improvement and by the customers' need in innovative decisions, Apple, Inc. must enlarge its R&D expenses. The company has necessary resources for considerable intensification in the R&D sphere:

- According to estimates of Oxfam America and New York Times, Apple, Inc. has accumulated between $181 billion and $236 billion in offshore accounts (Oxfam America, 2016; Drucker and Bowers, 2019).
- The company has quite a developed intellectual base for continuous innovative and technological development of its product line and service (Apple, Inc., 2019).

It should be noted that according to the PESTEL analysis, the main trend determining an industry development is customer centricity. The Five Forces analysis showed that customers have a "medium" power. However, inattention to their requirements and absence of new innovative and technological decisions can turn it into a real danger, and Apple, Inc. will start losing its customers and their loyalty. The information from section "Thinking" demonstrated that Apple, Inc. "does not listen to a customer's voice". Also, the lack of innovations negatively impacts the flagship net sales. As it appears from the PESTEL analysis information, the company must not only meet or anticipate the customers' requirements, but create effective communication channels with them, continuously analyze the customer's voice and consider it while creating its value proposition, build firm relationships based on the customers' trust. In other words, the company should be a customer-centered one.

The main conclusion is as follows:

- The differentiation strategy that constitutes the basis for customer value creation should be defined as the most effective one.
- The company's work in the R&D (research and development) sphere must be considerably enhanced; the result of this work will be continuous technological improvement of the products and services, as well as new innovative solutions, meeting or anticipating the customers' requirements.

- It is necessary not only to analyze and implement the customers' requirements, but to take a transition to a fully customer-centered company, having effective communications with the customers, creating long-term relationships based on trust for the company, exercising continuous analysis, and realization of the customers' requirements and their anticipation.

So, the somewhat corrected Apple, Inc. strategy is going to look like this:

1. **Market positioning:** a customer-centered innovative company (the strategy of differentiation).
2. **Creation of customer value:** unique products and services created on the basis of innovative technologies, an attractive brand image.

In sum, a considerable change is that Apple, Inc. does not simply analyze and meet the customers' requirements, but becomes a customer-centered company to a high degree, paying still more attention to innovations and technological improvement.

However, the company must also decide how it is going to organize its further development, think over its corporate strategy. Determining the corporate development strategy appears most advisable with the help of the Ansoff matrix (Ansoff, 1957). This matrix contains the following options: market penetration, product development, market development, and diversification. Let's consider each of the options.

Market penetration: It is thought to enlarge the market share at the current market. This can be achieved with the help of a high amount of products' sale to existing customers or of getting new customers at the current market.

Product development: Introduction of new products at the current market. It is necessary to think over the ways of introducing a new product to the customers and its ability to meet their requirements and outrival similar products of the company's competitors.

Market development: This strategy presupposes the discovery of new markets for existing products or products renovated with additional characteristics. Marketing research and segmentation will help in identifying new customers.

Diversification: This is entry into new markets with new products – the most risky strategy. The further an organization moves away from its traditional market and products, the more strength and resources it needs. However, if the current activities have become irrelevant such approach is quite righteous.

Definition of the corporate strategy on the basis of the Ansoff matrix
According to Galetto (2017), each year any business loses 20% in the average, even if the customers are satisfied with the company. Thus, customers must be continuously replenished. As the data from section "Thinking" showed, unlike Apple, Inc. its competitors enlarged their shares at the premium smartphone market; this is another evidence of a highly intensive competition in this branch, according to the Five Forces analysis.

Consequently, Apple, Inc. must continuously step up its market presence, choosing market penetration as its development strategy, with the help of selling a great amount of products to existing customers and of finding new ones at the current market; this will also have a positive influence on the company's net sales. As the Apple's main market is, first of all, found at the economically attractive regions, the task does not seem too difficult, on condition that the renovated business strategy is followed; and this strategy presupposes the development of customer centricity with a stronger accent on innovativeness and technical upgrading.

Conclusion: To denote the market penetration strategy to enlarge the market share at the current market as the strategy of further development.

The analysis of the company's portfolio showed that Apple, Inc. has rather a balanced product and service portfolio that allows generating the necessary economic value. However, the analysis also demonstrated that the market share of iPad is reducing. Besides, the company has only one flagship product – the iPhone, generating 55% of net sales, and the reduction of its sales will have its immediate negative influence on the company.

Consequently, under these conditions it is necessary to exercise the analysis of the product line broadening, with the help of a product which will be in great demand with the customers – following the diversification strategy. One of such products could be the TV-set. The facts show that the demand on this appliance will remain consistently stable. For instance, the number of households with SvoD (subscription video on demand) will grow from 250 mln. in 2018 to 450 mln. in 2022 (Watson, 2019). Simultaneously, the scale of *"pay TV households worldwide"* is growing in the whole world. If in 2017 it numbered 1.64 billion, in 2018 this number reached *"1.67 billion pay TV households worldwide"* (Watson, 2019).

It is noted that the TV-set market is rather saturated (Tankovska, 2020b). However, it is possible to guess that the customers will be rather glad if a new unusual appliance appears at this market. Certainly, a TV-set is not the most innovative product, but it possesses integration into the Apple ecosystem, and this fact will add to its characteristics, which will create an additional value for the company's customers. For instance the company will be able to sell TV-sets with a simultaneous subscription for Apple TV (a subscription streaming service), providing enough cloud space for storing films, personal videos and audios, accompanied by exclusive design and, probably, new technological or innovative solutions. It is noted that the Smart TV technology is becoming an ever-more-popular peculiarity of contemporary TV-sets, allowing the users to go online and connect to other appliances (Tankovska, 2020b). Additional "force" to the new product will be supplied by the Apple brand.

A new TV-set must also be positioned as the Apple, Inc. product having unique technological decisions. In other words, it will be meant for people who need a top-quality product, with unique characteristics, for whom its premium price will not be an obstacle.

Despite the fact that this diversification strategy is the riskiest, the presented data on the stable demand for this product, as well as Apple's experience in creating new products, minimize the risks of entering new markets.

Thuswise, the corporate strategy will considerably enforce the company's business strategy by its brand, market penetration, and product development.

So, at this stage the formation of Apple's business and corporate strategy is fully completed.

Business Strategy

1. **Market positioning:** customer-centered and innovative company (the strategy of differentiation).
2. **Creation of customer value**: unique products and services, developed on the basis of innovative technologies, and the attractive brand image.

Corporate Strategy

* **Market penetration:** customer acquisition and proposition broadening for existing customers at the company's traditional markets.
* **Diversification:** entry into new markets by means of creating a new product – the Apple TV-set.

Therefore, after Apple's business and corporate strategies have been formulated, the following section contains the definition of goals that facilitate their realization.

Constituent 4: Goals

Having defined the business and corporate strategies, it is necessary to denote the goals owing to which the company's further business strategy development and the realization of its corporate strategy could be possible.

It is worth noting that *"the goal is a specific formulation of something that we would like to accomplish over a defined period and taking into account the constraints of resources, cost etc..."* (da-Silva, 2016).

Correct formulation of goals will determine the success of the strategy realization and, consequently, the future of the company itself.

The goals aimed at further business strategy creation.

Market positioning: a customer-centered innovative company (the strategy of differentiation).

Creation of customer value: unique products and services created on the basis of innovative technologies, an attractive brand image.

As it can be seen from the formulated business strategy, its basis is customer centricity, innovativeness, technological development, which make the foundation for the creation of unique products and strengthen the attractiveness of the Apple, Inc. brand.

Consequently, the goal facilitating the business strategy realization can be formulated in the following ways: to provide the development of customer centricity, innovativeness, continuous technological development of the products, as well as the strengthening of the Apple brand.

This example shows that the goal is focused on options that are critically important for the strategy realization. In this case these are customer centricity, innovativeness, technological development, and the brand.

The goals aimed at the corporate strategy realization:

The Market penetration strategy: Customer acquisition and proposition broadening for existing customers at the company's traditional markets.

Please note the following circumstance: for the full realization of this strategy attention should be paid not only to customer acquisition but also to customer retention. This is connected to a simple fact that the scale of the customer base cannot be enlarged only by acquiring new customers, without retention of the existing ones. Besides, the following facts should be paid attention to:

•   Reichheld (2001) focuses on the idea that in 2001 in the financial sector, for instance, *"return customers tend to buy more from a company over time"*.
•   Companies spend from 5 to 25 times more money on customer acquisition than on customer retention (Gallo, 2014).

Thuswise, the goal directed to the achievement of the market penetration strategy will look like this: to provide more active sales of the already existing services and products, it is necessary to provide both customer acquisition and customer retention.

It is crucial to add that the achievement of this goal also depends on Apple's success in developing customer centricity and innovativeness, continuous technological improvement, which this business strategy presupposes.

Diversification strategy: Entry into new markets by means of creating a new product – the Apple TV-set.

In this case it is important to determine the goal allowing the start of the diversification strategy realization – introduction of a new product, the Apple TV-set:

•   To ensure the creation of Apple's new product – a TV-set, which is harmoniously built into the company's service ecosystem.

Besides, the formulated goals must undergo expert appraisal before they are finally adopted. All goals must be specific, measurable, attainable, realistic, and timed (Santangelo, 2013).

•   **Specific:** The goal must be definite, as it enhances the likelihood for it to be achieved. The definiteness of the goal means that in the process of goal's setting the result to be achieved is specified quite clearly and definitely.
•   **Measurable:** The goal must be sizeable as definite criteria are concerned, those which enable judging about the success of its achievement. It is necessary to choose indicators that demonstrate the process of the goal achievement.

- **Attainable:** Goals must be real for achievement, as the feasibility of the task performance depends on the individual contributor's motivation.
- **Relevant:** The understanding of the goal's contribution into the solution of the company's global tasks. In the event that the goal does not facilitate the company's development, such goal is useless.
- **Time-bound:** The goal's performance must be given time limits. This means that the final term must be determined, over which the goal should be considered unperformed. The time frame must be realistic.

Appraisal of Business Strategy Goals

Goal: To provide the development of customer centricity, innovativeness, continuous technological improvement of the products, as well as the strengthening of the Apple, Inc. brand.

Specific

The goal contains definite indicators, the achievement of which will allow the company's business strategy realization: the development of customer centricity, innovativeness, continuous technological improvement of the products, as well as the strengthening of the Apple brand.

Measurable

The achievement of this goal can be traced by quite definite indicators:

- The level of the company's customer satisfaction is sensibly measured by such indicators as the customer churn rate (the number of customers who stopped cooperating with the company) and the net promoter score (the percent of the customers ready to recommend the company's product or service).
- The force of the Apple brand can be traced by means of Interbrand Company's ratings.
- Innovativeness and technical development are determined by the presence of innovative solutions, technological improvement of the products and services, which influenced the positive dynamics of Apple's net sales.

Achievable

Factors denoting the goal achievement:

- The company currently holds a broad collection of intellectual property rights relating to certain aspects of its hardware devices, accessories, software, and services.
- Apple Company possesses all necessary innovative skills, technical competence, and marketing abilities of its personnel.
- The company actively engages third parties to develop its innovativeness.

Relevant

The goal completely corresponds to the company's business strategy aimed at the creation of value customer proposition, based on customer centricity, innovativeness, and a strong brand. Two key trends preconditioning the industry development – customer centricity and innovations' and technologies' development – have been considered.

Time Bound

The goal to be sought should be achieved at the earliest possible that allows quality realization. A full-year cycle is suggested as the basis.

Appraisal of Corporate Strategy Goals

Market Penetration Strategy

Goal: To provide more active sales of the existing services and products, it is necessary to provide both customer acquisition and customer retention.

Specific

The goal fully corresponds to the corporate strategy, pointing to the fact that sales' broadening of the company's products and service is possible on condition of both customer acquisition and customer retention.

Measurable

Since 2017 up to the first quarter of 2019 the share of Apple's nearest competitors at Premium Smartphone Segment Market Share was enlarged (PESTEL):

- Samsung enlarged its market presence from 23% to 25% – a 2% growth.
- Huawei enlarged its market presence from 8% to 16% – an 8% growth.

Apple's share at the Premium Smartphone Segment Market Share dropped from 58% to 47% within the same period. Loss of market constituted 11%.

It is assumed that Apple, Inc. will enlarge its share at the Premium Smartphone Segment Market by at least 5% with maximum gain.

Besides, it will be possible to measure the realization success of the market penetration strategy by the growth of the number of customers in the company.

Achievable

On condition of fulfillment of the goals related to customer centricity development, the growth of innovativeness rate and of technological leadership, this goal is quite achievable, as Apple, Inc. has an adequate potential, a strong brand, conditioned by the customers' trust and loyalty.

Relevant

The goal's realization will facilitate the elimination of losses connected with the natural customer churn and will broaden the company's customer base, which doubtlessly produce a positive influence on the realization of the market penetration strategy and on the total net sales rate.

Time Bound

There are good reasons to take a full-year period as the most realistic term of the goal realization.

Strategy of Diversification

Goal: To ensure the creation of Apple's new product – a TV-set, which is harmoniously built into the company's service ecosystem.

Specific

This goal is quite definite, as it clearly denotes the development of diversification strategy.

Measurable

The success of this product can be evaluated by its ability to generate net sales for the company. Taking into consideration the fact that a TV-set is a more bulk product than Mac or iPad, its net sales rate must be higher than of those products.

XIAOMI (2018:12) notes, *"during the year ended December 31, 2018, the global shipments of our smart TVs was 8.4 million units, representing a 225.5% year-on-year growth"*.

Considering Apple's potential, the suggested indicator is more than simply realistic. However, at this stage the issue of the initial creation of the TV-set is being considered. This goal is also quite measurable – having a TV-set ready for serial production.

Achievable

The following factors denote the achievability of goals:

* The customers' loyalty and a strong brand.
* The Company currently holds a broad collection of intellectual property rights relating to certain aspects of its hardware devices, accessories, software, and services.
* Apple possesses all necessary innovative skills, technical competence, and marketing abilities of its personnel.
* The company exercises active third-party engagement to develop its technological base.

Relevant

Factors defining the relevance of the goals:

* The competitive fitness of Apple, Inc. completely depends on its ability to ensure a continuing and timely introduction of innovative new products, services, and technologies to the marketplace.
* The company also receives a unique possibility to enter into the industry, which is new for it, broadening in this way its market presence.
* The TV-set can be harmoniously built into the company's service ecosystem.

Thus, the new Apple's product will provide the customers with still more possibilities for communication with the company. This will certainly strengthen the customer bonds and will have a positive influence on the company's financial soundness.

Time Bound

The development of the first iPhone started in 2004 and the gadget entered into the market in 2007.

Considering today's potential of Apple, the existence of necessary investment resources, the preliminary task of a TV-set development, and its implementation into the service system could be solved within a year's term, and in another half-year the series production of Apple TV-set and its offtake to the customers could be started.

So, the goals underwent the necessary expert investigation, and there exist all reasons to characterize them as real and achievable, facilitating Apple's business and corporate development strategies (Table 3.5).

Table 3.5 Joint table ("Goals")

GOALS
Business strategy
Market positioning: a customer-centered innovative company (the strategy of differentiation).
Creation of customer value: unique products and service created on the basis of innovative technologies, an attractive brand image.
Goal: To provide the development of customer centricity, innovativeness, continuous technological development of the products, as well as the strengthening of the Apple brand.
Corporate strategy: market penetration
Customer acquisition and proposition broadening for existing customers at the company's traditional markets.
Goal: to provide more active sales of the already existing services and products, it is necessary to provide both customer acquisition and customer retention.
Corporate strategy: diversification
Entry into new markets by means of creating a new product – the Apple TV-set.
• **Goal:** to ensure the creation of Apple's new product – a TV-set, which is harmoniously built into the company's service ecosystem.

Constituent 5: Risks

In this section, the risks that can interfere with the achievement of the goals facilitating the realization of the business and corporate strategies are identified and analyzed (Epstein and Buhovac, 2006; Passenheim, 2014). Deloitte (2013) notes that strategic risks are those risks that can produce the greatest impact on the company's ability of its strategy's realization.

Besides, evaluation of risks will be conducted and the reaction on them will be developed. It is impossible to avoid risks, that is why the best approach to managing them is identification and control (Nicholas and Steyn, 2012).

To identify risks, it is necessary to pay attention, first of all, to the goals facilitating the strategy realization and to determine the factors that can have a negative impact on their realization.

For instance, at the previous stage the following goal was identified:

- To provide conditions facilitating the realization of the business strategy: the development of customer centricity, innovativeness, continuous technological improvement of the products and services.

Consequently, the lack of company's actions facilitating the development of "customer centricity, innovativeness, technological improvement" can set the business strategy realization at stake, because the given options constitute its basis. Besides, without the development of these options it will be greatly difficult to exercise the market activity aimed at strengthening the company's brand, and also to realize the corporate strategy.

The information included under the sections "Thinking" and "Analyzing" also deserves paying attention to. For instance, the PESTEL analysis showed that the smartphone industry was influenced by the political factor. As the stakeholder analysis demonstrated, the government has rather a high power as the company is concerned, and can produce a negative impact on its activity.

Identification of risks can have rather a subjective character. So, the best approach aimed at identification of risks and managing them is brainstorming (Maley, 2012).

As soon as the risks are identified, they must undergo a series analysis, their impact rate on the company's ability to realize its strategy must be evaluated, and the reaction to the risks must be defined.

It is suggested to exercise risk evaluation according to the following scale:

- No risk
- Minor risk
- Moderate risk
- High risk

Corresponding to the risk evaluation, one or the other reaction is expected:

- No risk – no impact, no actions are needed.
- Minor risk – the impact is unimportant, actions are to the discretion of the company.
- Moderate risk – presents a threat for the strategy realization, requires additional resources and actions.
- High risk – the existence of the company is at stake, as well as its ability to realize the selected strategy; requires considerable resources and immediate actions.

Identified Risks

Risk: Absence of considerable innovations and technological solutions.
   Source of information: Section "Thinking", the PESTEL Analysis
   Innovative technological solutions, in Apple's product or service, is a key factor of realization of the company's strategy, its market positioning. Their absence produces a negative impact on the creation of the customer value proposition and the development of customer centricity, which makes a negative influence on the company's financial success.

Evaluation

The company continues to generate an imposing net sales amount; however, in 2019 the sagging of this indicator is noted by 2%, as compared to 2018; and the sagging of the iPhone net sales is 14%. The absence of considerable innovations and technological solutions can only strengthen this tendency. Hence, for the present moment, as the company generates rather impressive net sales, the risk related to the absence of considerable innovative solutions should be evaluated as **moderate**.

Reaction

The investments' growth in R&D, continuous attention to technical improvement and innovative solutions, introduction of the customer-centered approach.

Risk: Ignoring of the "Customer centricity" trend
Source of information: PESTEL, section "Thinking"

Customer centricity is one of the main trends defining the development of the smartphone industry. In the event of ignoring this trend, Apple, Inc. is running the risk of losing its market leadership. The analysis showed that theoretical research and practical activity of Apple's closest competitors demonstrate that customer centricity is the warrant of successful development and of profit maximization.

Evaluation

Information from section "Thinking" showed that the company does not exercise the proper analysis of the customers' requests, which produces a negative impact on its financial results. However, as the company's total net sales are still rather impressive, this risk can be evaluated as a **moderate** one. Without real actions the estimate "moderate" has all chances of growing into "high".

Reaction

It is advisable to actively inculcate the customer-centered approach, aimed at continuous monitoring of the customers' needs, their implementation, continuous communications on the "customer–company" level, with the purpose of creating long-term relations based on trust.

Risk: Negative influence of political factors.
Source of information: PESTEL, the Five Forces analysis, the stakeholder analysis.

There is the danger of political tension between the USA and China. This can find its reflection on Apple's industrial capacities, which, according to the information of the stakeholder analysis, are also placed in China. If the company ignores this risk, its ability of timely meeting the customer demand for its products can be imperiled because of the possible sanctions.

Besides, huge fines can be imposed, related to the failure to comply with the legislative requirements of the countries where Apple exercises its activity.

Evaluation

It is necessary to note that the company, according to the Five Forces analysis, tries to diversify its production capacities, re-establishing them to third countries. Besides, during the whole politically tense period between the two countries there was not a single case when it had a negative influence on Apple's production output. This can be explained by the fact that production capacities of many countries are situated in China, and this country is not interested in the creation of negative conditions that could facilitate the investors' outflow.

However, because of unpredictable nature of political processes' development, this risk must be evaluated as a **moderate** one.

Reaction

A continuous monitoring of legislations of the countries is necessary, which can produce the greatest impact on the company's activity, with the purpose of sanctions' non-admission. Special attention should be paid to political relations between the USA and the key countries where the company operates. The diversification of production capacities should be continued.

Risk: Impact of the COVID 19 pandemic on the smartphone market.
Source of information: PESTEL.

Because of the pandemic, the smartphone market in the USA, which is one of the key countries for Apple, reduced by 20% in the average. Apple, Inc. was obliged to shut down its offline stores on a worldwide scale. Besides, there exists the information that global key economies are starting to restore themselves after the pandemic. The GDP per capita dynamics up to 2019 in the world and in the regions which are of key importance for Apple, Inc. showed the incremental increase.

Evaluation

As the world economy is demonstrating the signs of restitution, this risk can be evaluated as a moderate one. Besides, in favor of this evaluation, speaks the fact that the population of the regions, which are of key importance for Apple, Inc., has probably enough resources allowing not to feel the crisis's influence to the full and preserve its payment ability. However, the danger of a repeated pandemic remains.

Reaction

Apple, Inc. should exercise an attentive monitoring of the current situation and work out the necessary plan of actions that minimize the decrease of payment activity in the event of a lengthy pandemic or other threats, like wars, natural calamities, and so on.

After the risks have been identified and analyzed, it is necessary to make a summary table, as shown in Table 3.6. This table will help to better visualize the obtained information with the purpose of its application in the construction of the general strategic table of Apple, Inc.

The basic conclusion of this stage: Analysis of risks showed that all of them can be referred to the "moderate" category; so, overcoming

Table 3.6 Joint table ("Risks")

Identified risks	Scale	Reaction
Absence of considerable innovations and technological solutions.	**moderate**	The investments' growth in R&D, continuous attention to technical improvement and innovative solutions, introduction of the customer-centered approach.
Ignoring of the "Customer centricity" trend.	**moderate**	It is advisable to actively inculcate the customer-centered approach, aimed at continuous monitoring of the customers' needs, their implementation, continuous communications on the "customer-company" level, with the purpose of creating long-term relations based on trust.
Negative influence of political factors.	**moderate**	A continuous monitoring is necessary of legislations of the countries, which can produce the greatest impact on the company's activity, with the purpose of sanctions' non-admission. Special attention should be paid to political relations between the USA and the key countries for the company. The diversification of production capacities should be continued.
Impact of the COVID 19 pandemic on the smartphone market.	**moderate**	Apple, Inc. should exercise an attentive monitoring of the current situation and work out the plan of necessary actions which minimize the decrease of payment activity in the event of a lengthy pandemic or other threats, like wars, natural calamities, etc.

them requires additional resources and efforts. For instance, the rise in innovativeness and technological improvement level requires considerable financial and intellectual resources; the same can be said about the development of client centricity, diversification of industrial capacities, combatting the pandemic aftereffects, in case it continues.

Ignoring these risks will set at stake the realization of the strategy of Apple, Inc., the main points of this strategy being customer centricity, raising of technological development level, and innovativeness. Consequently, it is necessary to pay the closest attention to managing identified risks, to conduct necessary investments in the further development.

Constituent 6: Actions

After solving the question with risks, bearing potential danger to the company's strategy and development, it is advisable to deal with actions aimed at the achievement of the goals facilitating the realization of business and corporate strategies. It should be noted that the company's strategy can be imitated by its competitors, but the actions leading to the strategy realization are much more difficult to repeat. All existing smartphones are, in fact, the iPhone's clones. However, the iPhone still remains a present-day leader, as no company has managed to imitate Apple's actions yet in creating this unique product and equally unique brand.

First and utmost, it is necessary to point out key notions used in the denoted goals and to define their interpretation. This will help to effectively form the necessary actions to achieve the goals.

Key Notions

- Innovations and technical improvement
- Customer centricity
- Brand development

These options produce an impact not only on the business strategy development; they directly influence the company's ability of realizing its corporate strategy.

For instance, without innovations and continuous technical improvement it will be impossible to realize the market penetration strategy, as it will be difficult to retain the current customers and acquire the new ones. This can be explained by the fact that innovations and technical improvement are the key points that attract the customers of Apple, Inc. and form the strength of its brand.

Innovations and Technical Improvement

The absolute difference between the two terms – "innovations" and "technical improvement" – was emphasized by Jack Welch (Welch and Welch, 2005) who noted that companies must continuously think about innovations and technical development. Drucker (2008) paid attention to the fact that one of business's main tasks is being innovative, as only owing to innovativeness continuous economic growth and development can be ensured. According to Drucker (2008), *"the most productive innovation is a different product or service creating a new potential of satisfaction, rather than an improvement"*. For instance the first iPhone is a bright example of an innovative decision. Owing to the unique smartphone, a customer value proposition was formed, which was transformed into a "pub" economic category in the form of continuously growing net sales. Thus, innovations are the creation of a product or service which was never proposed before. Thus, to innovations there can be referred the creation of a product or service which was never proposed before, the innovative technological solution which will bring a considerable unique customer value and economic profit for the company. Technological improvement is the improvement of an already existing product or service. The first iPhone is an innovative smartphone, and a three camera iPhone is its technological improvement.

A continuously improved product or service, generating the necessary value, will allow the company to have customers. A really innovative unique and unconventional solution will present a chance for the company to obtain really devoted customers. Hence, it is innovative solutions that allow creating long-term bonds with the customers, which will have a favorable impact on the company's financial indicators.

Conclusion: While planning actions aimed at the strategy realization, it is necessary to differentiate between innovativeness and technical improvement, placing emphasis on innovative decisions.

Customer Centricity

In this case it is necessary to determine the notion of customer centricity. The presence of customer centricity means the following (Aliekperov, 2021):

- Customer-centered personnel who is ready to promptly meet the customers' requests and solve the current problems.
- Continuous analysis of the customer's voice with the purpose of improving the existing products and services.

- Creation of steady customer relations based on trust and continuous proposition of value solutions meeting or anticipating the customers' requirements.
- Existence of communication channels that inform the customers about the advantages of cooperating with the company, and its products/services.
- Product or service presenting value for the customers, anticipating their expectations.
- Continuous measuring of the company's customer centricity rate, with the purpose of improvement of the customer-centered approach, planning of customer centricity development.

Conclusion: A clear understanding of what customer centricity is will allow the optimal organization of the introduction of a customer-centered approach into business development.

Brand Development

The company's brand does not exist on its own; it is a full reflection of the company's actions. Thus, a full-fledged realization of the customer-centered approach, customer value propositions based on technical improvement and innovations will always be the foundation for the development of the company's brand. Discrepancies between the company's actions and its brand's positioning will be taken negatively; so, the customers' trust rate to the company's products and services will drop, which will produce a negative impact on its financial performance.

  Conclusion: Marketing activity as to brand development must be supplemented by definite company's actions in the sphere of customer centricity, innovativeness, and technological improvement of the product and service.

So, after the basic notions are adjusted, it is necessary to denote the main actions that will facilitate the achievement of the goals to meet, and consequently, of the adopted business and corporate strategies.

Business Strategy

Actions

Goal: To provide the development of customer centricity, innovativeness, continuous technological improvement of the products, as well as the strengthening of the Apple, Inc. brand.

ACTION: TO PROVIDE A HIGH CUSTOMER CENTRICITY RATE.

With the purpose of the provision of a high customer centricity rate it is suggested to implement a customer experience model (CXM) in the company. The main purpose of the model is the creation of a customer-centered company, in which any strategic decisions are taken with consideration of "a customer voice"; as the result, the company presents to its customers a unique experience facilitating the creation of long-term relations (Aliekperov, 2021).

This model consists of the following elements as shown in Table 3.7 (Aliekperov, 2021):

Introduction of the suggested model will allow structuring the work on enhancing customer centricity rate, denoting the development of necessary options that facilitate the creation of a customer-centered company. For more details about the model see the book Aliekperov,

Table 3.7 The Customer Experience Model

CXM	The main indicators
Internal marketing (customer-centered personnel and top management)	• Existence of the vision value and company's culture directed to the customer • Direct personnel's participation in CX creation and development. • The company's activity are determined by the "voice of the customer"
Product/service marketing (the presence of competitive product/service portfolio possessing customer value.)	• The existence of a product/service which is created on the basis of continuously developing technologies and innovative solutions, meeting the customers' requirement or exceeding them.
Integrated marketing (provision of continuous customers' cooperation with the company and its brand).	• Existence of communication channels with the customers; • Correspondence of information to the target audience's requirements; • Personalized customer propositions.
Relationship marketing (creation of stable customer bonds).	• Construction of effective cooperation with the customers aimed at their retention and acquisition, as well as with the stakeholders influencing the company's customer centricity rate.
Performance marketing (planning of and measuring the company's customer centricity rate)	• Planning of the creation of a customer-centered approach providing a high rate of customer experience and measuring of the actions' effectiveness aimed at the development of customer centricity.

Table 3.8 R&D expenditure

Company	R&D expenditure (USD, mln. in 2019)	% from net sales
Apple, Inc.	16 217	6
Samsung	17 500	8
Huawei	20 110	14

Sources: Apple, Inc. (2019), Huawei Company (2019), Samsung (2019), Tankovska, (2020a).

Adyl (2021), "The Customer Experience Model", New York (NY): Routledge.

Action: To provide continuous technological improvement of the product and service, to work out new innovative solutions.

The following actions must be taken:

1. To lift the spending on R&D

As can be seen from Table 3.8, composed from the 2019 data, Apple, Inc. is behind its closest competitors in R&D spending.

With the purpose of ensuring its technological and innovative leadership, Apple, Inc. should lift its R&D spending up to 15% of net sales. Therewith, the emphasis must be placed on the "development of new innovative solutions and products", but not only on technological improvement.

Attention should be paid to the following points:

- Continuous improvement of the smartphones' screen characteristics.
- Development of technologies aimed at improving shooting quality.
- Enhancing the comfort rate in the iPhone usage, especially while using the Internet.
- The iPhone design improvement: the iPhone's look must differentiate it at once by its elegance in its competitive range.
- Continuous increase in the iPhone opportunities with consideration of the users' personal interests.
- Working out and introducing technologies related to the users' safety.
- Working out and introduction of Artificial Intelligence–related technologies.
- The closest possible attention should be given to the continuous improvement of Apple's service ecosystem.

- To analyze the necessity of a new-format smartphone creation, to be used in the satellite communication system within the projects Starlink and Kuiper.
- To analyze the necessity of the start of work at a smartphone supporting the standard next to 5G.

Action: To provide the company's brand development

- The Apple brand development must be aimed both at customer retention and customer acquisition.
- The emphasis must be placed on timely customer informing of technological changes in the company's products, of innovative solutions.
- To strengthen the company's personal customer communications.

These actions must be reflected in a specially developed program aimed at strengthening the Apple brand and correlate with customer centricity development.

Corporate Strategy

Actions

MARKET PENETRATION STRATEGY

Goal: To exercise customer acquisition as well as to enlarge the sales amount using current customers with the purpose of the broadening the traditional market.

Actions

- To determine the requirements of people who do not have iPhones, the performance of which would facilitate their purchasing Apple's smartphones.
- To determine the requirements of people who have iPhones, the performance of which would facilitate their purchasing more company's products and services.
- To analyze the possibility of these requirements' performance.
- To begin their realization.
- To boost the company's marketing activity aimed at the enlargement of the customers' number and retention of current customers.

DIVERSIFICATION STRATEGY

Goal: To provide the creation of a new Apple product – a TV-set, harmoniously built into the company's service ecosystem.

Actions

Primarily, it is necessary to decide how the work at the product's development and manufacturing will be exercised, as Apple, Inc. hasn't produced TV-sets before, so it does not comprise a relevant department. Three variants to solve this issue are suggested:

1. To purchase an existing TV-set manufacturer.
2. To entrust the existing company department with the development of a new project, responsible for MAC output.
3. To create a new department.

The option evaluation of the most acceptable alternative can be exercised according to the pros and cons principle.

To purchase an existing TV-set manufacturer

> **Pros** – the company will receive off-the-shelf technologies, approved manufacturer, and marketing of products.
>
> **Cons** – there is a strong possibility that the customers will not accept a new TV-set as Apple's original product. Besides, with a high probability, there will be no company at the market, corresponding to Apple's high standards.

To entrust the existing company department with the development of a new project, responsible for MAC output

> **Pros** – the work will start without delay, the employees, having the necessary professional experience, know all the company's requirements and standards very well.
>
> **Cons** – there is a strong possibility that the department, responsible for MAC output, will be unable to effectively combine two directions; this will have a negative influence on both the products.

To create a new department for the development of Apple's TV-set

> **Pros** – a new department will consist of specialists with the necessary experience and practical skills, which will help in starting the work at the project immediately.

Cons – the project's success will depend on how swiftly a leader will be found to head the new project and create an effectively cooperating team.

Thus, the third alternative as to creating a separate department will be an optimal one, because such a department will completely focus on the new project. The negative side of the points connected with successful cooperation of new team members can be successfully overcome by the people with common values and the wish to achieve the target goal.

Then it should be determined, owing to which innovative, technological, image-building solutions Apple, Inc. will be able to suggest its best possible value proposition to its customers, differentiating it in its competitive range.

Hence, the realization of the diversification strategy must be started with the following actions:

- To create a sub-department to manage the development of the new product.
- To define the customers' requirements and the existing competitors' solutions in the TV-set manufacturing sphere.
- To shape the plan of further actions, aimed at the creation of a new product – a TV-set – including the necessary resources and the main stages of the works.

All denoted actions must be joined into one table (Tables 3.9 and 3.10), for their clear presentation:

Thus, the main strategic actions are determined. In addition, on the operational level, the plan on realization of the company's strategy will be developed and exercised. For instance, it was determined on the strategic level that it is necessary to create a new department for the rollout of a new product – a TV-set. Consequently, already on the operational level the structure of this department will be defined, with consideration to the fact that in a year the first production prototype of the TV-set must be ready.

Constituent 7: Monitoring

After the strategy – including goals and actions – has been definitively shaped, it is necessary to determine the ways of its monitoring. Drucker (2008) emphasized that the company's efforts, spent on the control of its activity, are really investments into the future development. Owing

Table 3.9 Joint table "Actions" (Business strategy)

Business strategy

Goal:

To provide the development of customer centricity, innovativeness, continuous technological improvement of the products, as well as the strengthening of the Apple, Inc. brand.

Actions

Customer centricity

- To introduce in the company a customer experience model (CXM), this will be the foundation of customer centricity principles' realization.

Innovativeness and technical development

- to enlarge R&D investments – 15% of net sales, therewith the emphasis must be placed on the development of new innovative solutions and products.

Attention should be paid to the following points:

- continuous improvement of smartphone screens' characteristics;
- development of technologies, aimed at the improvement of shooting quality;
- upgrading of iPhone usage comfort level, especially of Internet usage;
- design improvement. The main purpose is comfort for users and the unique difference from the competitors' smartphones. The iPhone's look must instantly differentiate it in its competitive range;
- continuous broadening of possibilities of the iPhone personalization, with consideration to the users' interests.
- development and introduction of technologies related to the users' safety;
- development and introduction of technologies related to Artificial Intelligence;
- the closest attention to be paid to continuous improvement of Apple's service ecosystem;
- to analyze the necessity of smartphone creation, of a new format, to be used in the system of satellite communication within the Starlink and Kuiper projects.
- to analyze the necessity of the start of work at a smartphone, supporting the standard next to 5G.

Brand

- the Apple brand development must be aimed at both customer retention and customer acquisition;
- it is necessary to place the emphasis on timely customers' informing of technological changes in the company's products, of innovative solutions;
- personal customer communications in the company should be strengthened.

---

to the control of the strategy realization, the company can evaluate its effectiveness, can undertake necessary timely measures to correct the situation, allow for the mistakes made for their possible repetition to be excluded.

Table 3.10 Joint table "Actions" (Corporate strategy)

Corporate strategy

Market penetration strategy

Goal: to provide more active sales of the existing services and products it is necessary to provide both customer acquisition and customer retention.

Actions:
- To define the requirements of people who do not possess iPhones, the performance of which would facilitate their purchasing Apple smartphones;
- To define the requirements of people who possess iPhones, the performance of which would facilitate their purchasing new company's products or services;
- To analyze the possibility of performing these requirements and to start their implementation;
- To intensify the company's marketing activity, aimed at customer acquisition and customer retention.

Diversification strategy

Goal: to ensure the creation of Apple's new product – a TV-set, which is harmoniously built into the company's service ecosystem.

Actions:
- to create a sub-department to manage the development and marketing of the new product;
- to define the customers' requirements and the existing competitors' solutions in the sphere of TV-set manufacturing;
- to shape the plan of further actions, aimed at the creation of a new product – a TV-set – including the necessary resources and the main stages of the works.

On the strategic level, it is advisable to control the achievement of the goals, which provide the realization of the company's business and corporate strategies.

For instance, the goal facilitating the realization of the business strategy consists in the development of customer centricity, innovativeness, continuous technological improvement of the products and services, as well as in strengthening the Apple brand.

Therefore, it is necessary to conduct the monitoring of:

- customer centricity development;
- progress in the sphere of the products' and service's technological improvement;
- presence of innovative solutions;
- the brand's "force".

The control of the realization of actions should be passed over to the operation level. On the basis of the denoted actions, already on the operation level, the optimal plan of the strategic goals' achievement will be determined.

For effective monitoring of the strategy realization, it is suggested to divide all indicators into two groups: KPI and Metrics.

- KPI is the index that allows learning how effective the company's efforts, aimed at the achievement of the desired goal, were (Alsadeq and Hakam, 2010).
- Metrics are the indicators that allow to track the work output and progress in the process of the goal's achievement (O'Hara and Ginger, 2000).

As the main goal of the strategy is to ensure economic value, total net sales and products' net sales are suggested as the basic KPI. This indicator is the most important criterion of the company's strategy effectiveness. It is necessary to note that the success of the strategy should not be measured by the indicator of net income. This can be explained by the fact that net income formation is influenced by the combination of various factors, such as the sum of paid taxes, expenses related to manufacturing of products and creation of services. Consequently, on the operational level, the total net sales obtained owing to the strategy realization is converted into net income. This is a very important moment, which must be constantly within the eyesight of the company's management, as the operational level, on which the strategy's realization takes place, creates, in the long run, the necessary economic value. **It is necessary to underline that the success of any company is determined by its ability to provide a constant growth of net sales and net profit consequently. It is the first and foremost condition of sustained development.**

In 2019 Apple's total net sales was USD 260,174 mln., and its net income was USD 55,256 mln. (Apple, Inc., 2019).

In view of the circumstance that the world economy, according to the information of the PESTEL, is beginning to recover and the company is going to enhance its R&D activity, it is sensible to pledge the total net sales growth of Apple, Inc. as 8–10%, with possible maximum growth of this indicator. The facts that the total sales growth from 2016 to 2018 constituted in the average 23% speak in favor of this prognosis (Apple, Inc., 2019). Besides, according to the PESTEL, the growth of total net sales can also be observed in 2020. It is the updated Apple's business strategy that must provide the total net sales growth, as it presumes

Table 3.11 Total net sales and net sales of the products\services of Apple, Inc.

Net sales	Projection
iPhone	5–8%
MAC	3–5%
iPad	2–5%
Service	15–25%
Wearables, Home, and Accessories	40–45%
Total net sales	**8–10%**

the development of customer centricity, the growth of attention to innovations, and technological improvement.

So, it is suggested to define the total net sales in the amount of 8–10% with possible maximum growth of this indicator. Thereat, it is also necessary to pay attention to the net sales of the company's products and services (Table 3.11).

Projections' Feasibility

iPhone (Apple, Inc., 2019): In the period between 2018 and 2019, the iPhone net sales dropped by 14%. However, in the period between 2017 and 2018 this product's net sales demonstrated the growth by 18%. Besides, according to the portfolio analysis data, the demand for smartphones will show a persistent global rise. It is supposed that the growth of attention to R&D will allow overcoming the negative tendency and increase of the net sales amount up to 5–8%.

MAC (Apple, Inc., 2019): Between 2018 and 2019 this product's net sales grew by 2%. However, the demand for computers, according to the portfolio analysis, will grow. The predicted net sales amount, considering the R&D expense growth, can be defined at the rate of 3–5%, because the demand for the product still remains.

iPad (Apple, Inc., 2019): It should be noted that though in the period between 2018 and 2019 this product's net sales demonstrated a 16% growth, generally between 2014 and 2019 the product's net sales dropped by 42%. Besides, the demand for tablets, according to the information obtained from the portfolio analysis, continues to show a considerable decline. It is possible to suppose the possible growth of this product's net sales up to 2–3%.

Service (Apple, Inc., 2019): This category doubtlessly plays the leading role in the strategy realization, as the company's service ecosystem is one of the most important conditions of the customer's purchasing the company products. In 2019 the sales growth constituted 16%. The prediction can be defined as 15–25% net sales growth.

Wearables, Home, and Accessories: During the six months period, ended 2020, this category's sales volume grew by 31%. (Apple, Inc., 2020). In the period between 2018 and 2019 the growth constituted 41% (Apple, Inc., 2019). These products, according to the portfolio analysis, can be convincingly referred to the "stars" category. Hence, the growth between 40% and 45% can be predicted.

Tracing the net sales of each product regularly, the company will always be able to evaluate how correct its actions were and undertake the necessary efforts with the purpose of correcting them if the indicators get worse.

All other indicators will be referred to the metrics category, as in the long run they will directly influence the products' and the service's net sales and total net sales.

Monitoring of Business Strategy Realization

Customer Centricity Development

It is suggested to determine the rate of customer centricity development with the help of monitoring the customer churn rate and net promoter score indicators. The suggested indicators allow depicting the customers' satisfaction rate with the cooperation of the company and with its value proposition. However, only these ratios should not be relied upon, as they reflect the situation post factum. For instance, the customer churn rate showed that in three months after the start of the strategy realization the company lost a certain percent of its customers. However, the reasons of such customers' behavior had evidently appeared not on the day of data obtaining, but much earlier.

Consequently, it is necessary to continuously analyze the customer's voice, define negative tendencies before the situation started getting worse. With this purpose it is very important to organize bilateral digital communication channels that allow the customers' evaluation of the service rate and their satisfaction with the products. It is also useful to conduct focus groups with the customers for discussing various issues related to the relationships with the company.

Innovations and Technological Improvement Rate off the Products and Services

The measurement of this option is suggested with the help of the following indicators

- Number of developed and realized technological and innovative solutions.
- Realization rate and quality of the innovations and technological improvement program.

Strength of the Apple Brand

- Position in the Interbrand rating.
- Brand cost according to the Interbrand rating.
- Realization rate and quality of the program on the company's brand strengthening.

Monitoring of Corporate Strategy Realization

Market Penetration Strategy

- Growth of the customer base (percent).
- Market presence strengthening of premium smartphones at least by 5%.

Diversification Strategy

- Creation of a new product – a TV-set.

Within a year to exercise the launching of the first experimental copies and to prepare the start of full-scale manufacturing.

It is necessary to exercise a monthly evaluation on the course of works related to the preparation of the new product's creation.

It should be noted that the success of relationships with the stakeholders, influencing the strategy realization, must also be analyzed on a mandatory basis.

First of all, attention should be paid to suppliers, who supply necessary components. One of the variants is recurring questioning of their representatives with the purpose of defining how comfortable their cooperation is with Apple, Inc. and what is necessary to be done, in their opinion, for the improvement of this cooperation.

Besides, it is necessary to evaluate by a questionnaire the personnel's engagement in the strategy creation, how much the employees are informed of the company strategy, its goals, what should be changed, in their opinion.

The closest attention should also be given to competitors' activity. With this purpose it is sensible to work out key parameters to conduct the comparative analysis of Apple, Inc. and its competitors. For instance:

net sales rate on the products and total net sales, R&D expenses, the comparative analysis of the products' and service's characteristics, and so on. The main purpose of the analysis is understanding the competitors' activity, aimed at the provision of unconditioned technological and innovative leadership of Apples' products and services.

The assessment of media call-backs on the company's activity, observations about it in various regions and countries which help in evaluating the society opinion on Apple's activity.

Probably the easiest evaluation will be the evaluation of the relations with stakeholders who pay attention to the company's profitability and to the ways it is going to develop. This category will probably express their dissatisfaction with the company's work much earlier than other stakeholders will. It is advisable to control the company by managing the identified risks.

All the data to exercise monitoring should be reflected in one unified table (see Tables 3.12 to 3.15).

This table consists of the following sections:

1. KPI – monitoring the strategy's success.
2. METRICS – monitoring the goals and achievement which facilitate the realization of the business and corporate strategies.
3. Risks response monitoring.
4. Stakeholders relationships monitoring.

It is worth emphasizing once again that the aim of monitoring is not only to understand how successful the company's strategy is, but the timely reaction in case of negative tendency appearing in the indicators, lack of progress in realization of the desired plans, problems in stakeholder relationships, etc.

Table 3.12 Monitoring ("KPI")

KPI	
Net sales	*Projection*
iPhone	5–8%
MAC	3–5%
iPad	2–5%
Service	20–25%
Wearables, Home, and Accessories	40–45%
Total net sales	8–10%
Assessment periodicity: regularly	

Table 3.13 Monitoring ("Business and corporate strategies-metrics")

Risks response monitoring	
Absence of considerable innovations and technological solutions	To exercise assessment of the success of the program performance on technological improvement of the products and innovations. In case of lack of progress, instant taking correction measures to be exercised.
Risk related to ignoring of the "customer centricity" trend	To exercise assessment of the successful performance of the customer experience model implementation, as well as of indicators related to the change in the customer satisfaction rate. In case of the lack of progress in the development of the customer-centered approach and the facts of negative tendencies, correction measures to be taken.
Risk related to the negative influence of political factors	On a monthly basis to trace the political situation monitoring in the regions and countries which are the key ones for Apple, Inc. On a quarter-yearly basis to exercise a legislature monitoring of the countries which are the key ones for Apple, Inc. and to reveal considerable changes influencing the company's activity. Diversification of industrial capacities to be continued. In case of negative tendencies, instant taking correction measures to be exercised.
Risks related to repetition of the pandemic, to various natural calamities, war conflicts, etc.	It is necessary to analyze thoroughly the situation in the regions which are the key ones for the company with the purpose of working out an adequate reaction to a possible threat.

Table 3.14 Monitoring ("Risks")

Risks response monitoring	
Absence of considerable innovations and technological solutions	To exercise assessment of the success of the program performance on technological improvement of the products and innovations. In case of lack of progress, instant taking correction measures to be exercised.
Risk related to ignoring of the "customer centricity" trend	To exercise assessment of the successful performance of the customer experience model implementation, as well as of indicators related to the change in the customer satisfaction rate. In case of the lack of progress in the development of the customer-centered approach and the facts of negative tendencies, correction measures to be taken.
Risk related to the negative influence of political factors	On a monthly basis to trace the political situation monitoring in the regions and countries which are the key ones for Apple, Inc. On a quarter-yearly basis to exercise a legislature monitoring of the countries which are the key ones for Apple, Inc. and to reveal considerable changes influencing the company's activity. Diversification of industrial capacities to be continued. In case of negative tendencies, instant taking correction measures to be exercised.
Risks related to repetition of the pandemic, to various natural calamities, war conflicts, etc.	It is necessary to analyze thoroughly the situation in the regions which are the key ones for the company with the purpose of working out an adequate reaction to a possible threat.

Table 3.15 Monitoring ("Stakeholders")

Stakeholders relationships monitoring	
Suppliers	Survey as to the key suppliers' satisfaction with cooperation with Apple, Inc.
	Assessment periodicity: once in six months
Employees	Survey as to the employees' satisfaction with the work for the company and with their participation in the strategy creation and realization.
	Assessment periodicity: annually
Society	Tracing the society reaction on the activity of Apple, Inc. on the basis of the press and social networks publication and so on.
	Assessment periodicity: once in six months
Government	The analysis of cooperation rate with the governments of the countries which are the key ones for Apple, Inc. as to the absence of claims to the company's activity, the political situation monitoring.
	Assessment periodicity: on a monthly basis
Competitors	Regular analysis of the competitors' activity according to pre-defined criteria.
	Assessment periodicity: on a quarter-yearly basis
Shareholders	Analysis of the shareholders' opinions as to the activity of Apple, Inc.
	Assessment periodicity: annually, at the annual meeting of shareholders.

Strategic Table of Apple, Inc.

Thus, the work on the creation of the Apple, Inc. strategy can be considered to be completed; further on all the information must be passed over to the operation level for the outlined actions' realization, for organization of stakeholder relationships, the company's necessary actions as to the denoted risks. The control over the strategy's realization grounded on the information stated in section "Monitoring" must be exercised by the company's CEO and its top management on a mandatory basis.

Information on each stage of strategy creation on the basis of the TASGRAM system should be generated in the Strategic Table of Apple, Inc.

It is sensible to form this table from the following points:

- Business and corporate strategy, the main goals and actions;
- Risks;

- Stakeholder relationships;
- Monitoring.

This table will allow viewing the whole strategy of Apple, Inc. in a convenient manner for comprehension and analysis. Section on "Stakeholders" will give a unique opportunity to control the process of their impact on the realization of the company's strategy and to undertake the relevant measures, if necessary. Besides, the Strategic Table of Apple, Inc. will enable to optimally render the strategy to all employees and to receive the feedback in the form of suggestions aimed at the improvement of the suggested strategy.

Completing this chapter, it is necessary to emphasize once again that the strategy of Apple, Inc. was created with the help of the TASGRAM system (Tables 3.16 to 3.21), which can be graphically represented in the following way (Figure 3.5, p. 93)

Each section makes its special contribution into strategy creation. However, it is the first constituent, "Thinking", that allows obtaining the necessary information before the final formation of the strategy,

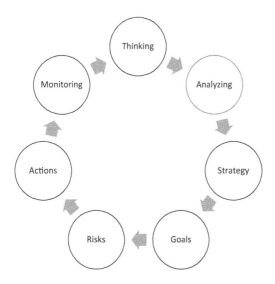

Figure 3.5 TASGRAM system.

Table 3.16 Strategic table of Apple, Inc. ("Business strategy")

Business strategy

Market positioning: customer-centered and innovative company (the strategy of differentiation);

Creation of customer value: unique products and service, developed on the basis of innovative technologies, the attractive brand image.

Goal, facilitating the strategy realization:

To provide the development of customer centricity, innovativeness, continuous technological improvement of the products, as well as the strengthening of the Apple, Inc. brand.

Actions

Customer centricity

- To introduce in the company a customer experience model, this will be the foundation of customer centricity principles' realization.

Innovativeness and technical development

- to enlarge R&D investments – 15% of net sales, therewith the emphasis must be placed on the development of new innovative solutions and products.

Attention should be paid to the following points:

- continuous improvement of smartphone screens' characteristics;
- development of technologies, aimed at the improvement of shooting quality;
- upgrading of iPhone usage comfort level, especially of Internet usage;
- design improvement. The main purpose is comfort for users and the unique difference from the competitors' smartphones. The iPhone's look must instantly differentiate it in its competitive range;
- continuous broadening of possibilities of the iPhone personalization, with consideration to the users' interests;
- to analyze the necessity of smartphone creation, of a new format, to be used in the system of satellite communication within the Starlink and Kuiper projects.
- to analyze the necessity of the start of work at a smartphone, supporting the standard next to 5G.
- development and introduction of technologies related to the users' safety;
- development and introduction of technologies related to Artificial Intelligence;
- the closest attention to be paid to continuous improvement of Apple's service ecosystem;

Brand

- the Apple brand development must be aimed at both customer retention and customer acquisition;
- it is necessary to place the emphasis on timely customers' informing of technological changes in the company's products, of innovative solutions;
- personal customer communications in the company should be strengthened.

Table 3.17 Strategic table of Apple, Inc. ("Corporate strategy")

Corporate strategy

Market penetration: customer acquisition and proposition broadening for existing customers at the company's traditional markets

---

Goal, facilitating the strategy realization:
To provide more active sales of the existing services and products it is necessary to provide both customer acquisition and customer retention.

Actions
• To define the requirements of people who do not possess iPhones, the performance of which would facilitate their purchasing Apple smartphones;
• To define the requirements of people who possess iPhones, the performance of which would facilitate their purchasing new company's products or services;
• To analyze the possibility of performing these requirements and to start their implementation;
• To intensify the company's marketing activity, aimed at customer acquisition and customer retention.

Diversification strategy: entry into new markets by means of creating a new product – the Apple TV-set.

Goal, facilitating the strategy realization:
To ensure the creation of Apple's new product – a TV-set, which is harmoniously built into the company's service ecosystem.

Actions
• To create a sub-department to manage the development and marketing of the new product;
• To define the customers' requirements and the existing competitors' solutions in the sphere of TV-set manufacturing;
• To shape the plan of further actions, aimed at the creation of a new product – a TV-set – including the necessary resources and the main stages of the works.

Table 3.18 Strategic table of Apple, Inc. ("Risks and Stakeholders")

RISKS

Identified risk: absence of considerable innovations and technological solutions.

Reaction: the investments' growth in RD, continuous attention to technical improvement and innovative solutions, introduction of the customer-centered approach.

Identified risk: ignoring of the "Customer centricity" trend.

(continued)

Table 3.18 Cont.

RISKS

Reaction: it is advisable to actively inculcate the customer-centered approach, aimed at continuous monitoring of the customers' needs, their implementation, continuous communications on the "customer-company" level, with the purpose of creating long-term relations based on trust.

Identified risk: negative influence of political factors.

Reaction: A continuous monitoring is necessary of legislations of the countries, which can produce the greatest impact on the company's activity, with the purpose of sanctions' non-admission. Special attention should be paid to political relations between the USA and the key countries for the company. The diversification of production capacities should be continued.

Identified risk: influence of COVID 19 pandemic on the smartphone market

Reaction: Apple, Inc. should exercise an attentive monitoring of the current situation and work out the plan of necessary actions which minimize the decrease of payment activity in the event of a lengthy pandemic or other threats, like wars, natural calamities, etc.

STAKEHOLDERS

Suppliers: high rate of influence on the company; close cooperation is necessary

Employees: high rate of influence on the company; close cooperation is necessary.

Community: influence rate on the company is not very expressed. Continuous informing of the society on socially important initiatives is necessary.

Government: influence rate on the company is quite expressed. It is necessary to trace that the company's activity is exercised within the legislative requirements.

Competitors: influence rate on the company is nonessential. Active monitoring of the competitors' activity is necessary.

Shareholders: high rate of influence on the company; close cooperation is necessary.

Table 3.19 Strategic table of Apple, Inc. ("Monitoring – KPI and Metrics: Business and Corporate strategies")

Monitoring	
KPI	
Net sales	**Projection**
iPhone	5–8%.
MAC	3–5%
iPad	2–5%
Service	20–25%

Table 3.19 Cont.

Monitoring

Wearables, Home, Accessories   40–45%.

Total net sales	**8–10%**

Assessment periodicity: regularly

Metrics

Business strategy

Customer centricity development

- Indicators: Customer churn rate and Net promoter score.
  Assessment periodicity: on a monthly basis
- Analysis of the data obtained in the course of the customers' evaluations by means of digital channels, of the company's service and products.
  Assessment periodicity: continuously
- Information obtained by conducting focus-groups aimed at the study of the customers' satisfaction rate with the company's products and service.
  Assessment periodicity: once in six months
- Assessment of the program performance on CXM implementation
  Assessment periodicity: on a monthly basis

Innovativeness and technological improvement

- Assessment of the program realization of the products' technological improvement, as well as the presence of innovative solutions
  Assessment periodicity: on a monthly basis

The Apple brand

- Position and value of the Apple brand in the Interbrand rating.
  Assessment periodicity: annually, on the basis of the Interbrand rating.
- Realization rate and quality of the program of the company's brand strengthening.
  Assessment periodicity: quarter-yearly

Corporate strategy

Market penetration strategy

- Dynamics of the customers number growth (%)
- To raise the market presence of premium class smartphones at least by 5%
  Assessment periodicity: the dynamics of these indicators' change to be traced on a quarter-yearly basis

Diversification strategy

- During the year to exercise the launch of the first experimental TV-sets and to prepare the start of the full-scale manufacture.
  Assessment periodicity: the progress in the new product's creation to be assessed on a monthly basis.

Table 3.20 Strategic table of Apple, Inc. ("Monitoring – Risks")

Risks	
Absence of considerable innovations and technological solutions	To exercise assessment of the success of the program performance on technological improvement of the products and innovations. In case of lack of progress, instant taking correction measures to be exercised.
Risk related to ignoring of the "customer centricity" trend	To exercise assessment of the successful performance of CXM implementation, as well as of indicators related to the change in the customer satisfaction rate. In case of the lack of progress in the development of the customer-centered approach and the facts of negative tendencies, correction measures to be taken.
Risk related to the negative influence of political factors	On a monthly basis to trace the political situation monitoring in the regions and countries which are the key ones for Apple, Inc. On a quarter-yearly basis to exercise a legislature monitoring of the countries which are the key ones for Apple and to reveal considerable changes influencing the company's activity. Diversification of industrial capacities to be continued. In case of negative tendencies, instant taking correction measures to be exercised.
Risks related to repetition of the pandemic, to various natural calamities, war conflicts, etc.	It is necessary to analyze thoroughly the situation in the regions which are the key ones for the company with the purpose of working out an adequate reaction to a possible threat.

Table 3.21 Strategic table of Apple, Inc. ("Monitoring – Stakeholders")

Stakeholders	
Suppliers	Survey as to the key suppliers' satisfaction with cooperation with Apple, Inc. **Assessment periodicity:** once in six months

Table 3.21 Cont.

Stakeholders	
Employees	Survey as to the employees' satisfaction with the work for the company and with their participation in the strategy creation and realization. **Assessment periodicity**: annually
Society	Tracing the society reaction on the activity of Apple, Inc. on the basis of the press and social networks publication and so on. **Assessment periodicity:** once in six months
Government	The analysis of cooperation rate with the governments of the countries which are the key ones for Apple, Inc. as to the absence of claims to the company's activity, the political situation monitoring. **Assessment periodicity:** on a monthly basis
Competitors	Regular analysis of the competitors' activity according to pre-defined criteria. **Assessment periodicity:** on a quarter-yearly basis
Shareholders	Analysis of the shareholders' opinions as to the activity of Apple, Inc. Assessment periodicity: annually, at the annual meeting of shareholders.

evaluating critically the current strategy or shaping the preliminary variant of a new strategy. Moreover, the given approach enables a considerable enhancing of the obtained conclusions' reliability as concerns the company's strategy. This can be explained with the following circumstance: at the "thinking" stage a preview version of the company's strategy is worked out, which later undergoes critical analysis after the information from section "Analyzing" is obtained. Consequently, the company gets a unique opportunity to analyze twice the correctness of the conclusions made, concerning its strategy.

Fisher and Scriven (1997) note that critical thinking includes interpretation and evaluation of observations, communications, information, and argumentation.

Thuswise, the initial cooperative critical discussion and evaluation of information, various argumentations, will help not only in shaping the strategy's preview variant for its further analysis, but will create the necessary synergy among various participants, facilitating more effective work on the final formation of the business and corporate strategies.

4 Questions and Answers

This chapter suggests questions and the answers to which provide a better idea of what the TASGRAM system is, and what are the optimal ways of using it. Other issues related to strategy creation will also be considered.

Why is TASGRAM Called the System of Strategy Creation?

It is necessary to note that a system consists of interconnecting elements that influence one another (Ackoff, 1999; Jackson, 2003). TASGRAM is also a set of interrelated elements. For instance, in Chapter 3, the section "Analyzing" contains the information that provides the basis for strategy, and further on, the goals, actions, and risks are determined which hinder the aims' realization, and consequently, hinder the strategy's realization.

Identification of TASGRAM as a system allows applying to it the rules appropriate to systems, and this makes its application more effective. Ackoff (1999) remarks that if changes took place in one part of the system, and they are not followed by changes in its other parts, this can ruin the whole system. In the event that the PESTEL analysis showed considerable changes in the drivers, determining the industry's development and this is not considered while the strategy is formed, this fact will challenge the system's effectiveness and, consequently, the company's ability to generate economic value. Therefore, any changes in the elements of the TASGRAM system of strategy creation must be analyzed as to their influence on the system as a whole.

Can the strategy creation system TASGRAM be used for the initial formation of an absolutely new strategy?
Yes, it can, and the work should start with the first step of the TASGRAM system of strategy creation – with "Thinking". Applying

the Porter Generic strategy, it is necessary to determine which strategy will be the basis of exercising the company's marketing positioning: differentiation, cost leadership, or focus. The customers' key requirements must be learned and it is necessary to think out the ways the value proposition will be formed on the basis of marketing positioning, what will make its uniqueness aimed at meeting or anticipating the clients' requirements. For instance, in Amazon Company there are variety of safe and quality goods and services, convenient ways of purchasing and delivery of these products.

Thus, a preliminary working theory of the business strategy can be formulated, with the use of the following scheme (Figure 4.1)

In addition, it is necessary to act according to the TASGRAM strategy creation system, i.e. to move to the "Analyzing" section in Chapter 3. Then, on the basis of the obtained information, one should analyze the preliminary strategy version, with the purpose of its approval or correction. The subsequent development of corporate strategy using the Ansoff matrix will determine the development of the business strategy.

Does the application of the TASGRAM strategy creation system guarantee that a strategy created on its basis will be successful and will provide the company's development and the necessary economic value?

No, the TASGRAM system cannot guarantee this. However, with the help of this system one can work out a preliminary version of a strategy, collect the necessary information which will help in affirming the truth of the chosen strategy, may be in correcting it or in forming a new strategy. Besides, the TASGRAM system will point to the need of risks evaluation, of determining and verification of the goals and actions needed for the strategy's realization, of considering stakeholders'

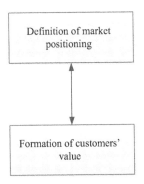

Figure 4.1 Schematical representation of business strategy.

requirements, and measuring the strategy's effectiveness. These options will allow a considerable enhancing of the created strategy's reliability, which will reinforce the probability of obtaining economic value needed for the company's development.

Under which conditions the strategy must necessarily be changed?
Significantly, the example with Apple, Inc. and the analysis of the situation with the iPhone net sales sagging by 14% and total net sales sagging by 2% in 2019 in the section "Thinking" in Chapter 3 showed that the reason is not the strategy, but the non-performance of the two fundamental conditions: technological and innovative development and meeting the customers' requirements. Consequently, before placing a question of strategy change, it is necessary to analyze if the conditions facilitating its realization are being fulfilled.

However, if following the current strategy doesn't create customer value, the company doesn't generate economic value necessary for its development, the strategy must be reconsidered. Thereat, the company should not learn about it after the fact, after the considerable drop of the demand on its products or services, and the net sales sagging. A continuous monitoring should be exercised as to the customers' satisfaction with the goods or services and the net sales dynamics, and in the event of the slightest falling-off, necessary measures should be taken for changing or correcting the strategy.

How is it possible to make provisions for the appearance of exterior force majeure circumstances and risks influencing the realization of the company strategy?

Whitley (2006) states that it is essential to make an emphasis on the fact that today's world is very unstable and unpredictable. Many researchers compare today's society with the world of quantum physics when it is impossible to foresee what will happen after the collision of two particles of the quantum world (Ramage and Shipp, 2009).

A vivid example is the situation with the pandemic caused by the COVID virus which was a total surprise for the whole world; it found its expression in the inability to define the adequate reaction to this threat at the initial stage.

For example, in the USA, reasons for not responding quickly to the threats were attributed to "technical flaws, regulatory obstacles, conventional bureaucracy, and lack of leadership at multiple levels" (Hindsley, 2020).

In the "The Global Risks Report 2020" the start of the pandemic was predicted twice, in 2007 and in 2008 (World Economic Forum, 2020). In 2020 in this report the risk related to the pandemic was not stated. This report was also published by the famous consulting company Mercer (no data). By this publication Mercer indirectly confirmed the reliability of "The Global Risks Report 2020".

As the above-mentioned example shows, companies dealing with analytics, in some cases cannot present true anticipation as to risks. Thuswise, it is most likely that it is impossible to anticipate all possible risks that can influence the company's strategy and its business. Besides, it should be considered that in the event of the pandemic's repetition there are no guarantees of its development according to the present scenario. Consequently, each time the company will have to work out a new unique reaction to a seemingly identical risk.

The risk for the company is also the incorrect identification of trends defining the industry development. In 1975, the 25-year-old Kodak company engineer Steven Sasson invented the first digital camera (Estrin, 2015). However, Kodak management's inability to see digital photography as a disruptive technology did not allow predicting the future trend, which determined the industry's development. This was one of the factors that ruined the film-based business model of Kodak Company (Estrin, 2015). It was shown in the Chapter 3 that all risks, force majeure were identified in the section "Risks" of the TASGRAM system with the help of the information of section "Analyzing".

For instance, owing to the PESTEL analysis, the main drivers were identified which determine the development of the smartphone industry: "customer centricity", and also "the development of innovations and technologies". Further on, in the section "Risks" in Chapter 3, the failure to follow these drivers was classified as the threat for Apple, Inc., influencing its ability to generate the necessary client value.

As mentioned above, according to Maley (2012), the optimal approach to risk identification is a brainstorming meeting. This approach will enable to lessen the factor of a subjective evaluation at risks' identification. However, for more effective brainstorming, it must be prepared.

With this purpose, exercising of the following arrangements is suggested:

- To define the brainstorming participants. Company's top management must be included on the mandatory basis.
- Each participant must conduct the PESTEL analysis, and on its basis draw out the most meaningful risks for the realization of the company's strategic goals.
- All materials must be directed to the employee responsible for the brainstorming, who will make a rank-ordered list of identified risks.
- This information is discussed with the brainstorm participants and the most meaningful risks for the realization of the company's strategy are determined.

Organization of brainstorming related to risks identification is mandatory before the start of the process of strategy revision or strategy creation, and later it is for consideration of the company's top management. However, the degree of probability of these or those risks must be continuously monitored by the corresponding business division.

Who is responsible for strategy creation?
The creation of the company strategy is a direct responsibility of its leader, CEO. However, Whitley (2006) emphasizes that it is impossible to persuade people in anybody's version of reality, because for them nothing is real unless they take part in its creation. Blanchard (2007) focuses attention on the fact that leadership is exercised not for people, but with people. Thus, the leader's task is the engagement of top management, the company personnel, probably its main stakeholders into the process of strategy creation. This can be the organization of strategic sessions which will include co-working at strategy creation, its approval and discussion of the obtained results.

It is absolutely necessary that the personnel is developed with the purpose of providing full understanding of what strategy is, which tasks it solves, what the process of company strategy creation is like.

Depending on the company's size, with the purpose of more effective work at the strategy, a special department – the Department of strategy creation and its realization monitoring – can be created.

How should the company personnel be provided information on its strategy?
For the full information provision of the employees on the company strategy, the strategic press release should be published, which would present the Strategic Table of Apple, Inc. and the ways it was created: brief conclusions of "Analyzing" chapter and so on. Threat, all employees should be given an opportunity of expressing their opinions as to the published document by means of a special digital channel. For instance, a special corresponding section is defined on the inner site, in which each employee can leave his/her suggestions and commentaries. Besides, the employees must be informed on the start of strategy creation work with the purpose of forehanded introduction of their suggestions.

This book introduced the Strategic Table of Apple, Inc. Can it be used as a real strategy of the Apple, Inc.?
It should be emphasized that this table was worked out for educational purposes to demonstrate the capacities of the TASGRAM system. However, it could be certainly suggested for Apple, Inc. as a strategy, on condition that Apple's top management would take part in its creation,

all necessary insider information on the company's opportunities would be provided, as well as the company's statistics. Thereat, the emphasis should be placed on the fact that the suggested strategy was created on the basis of the information taken from reliable open sources, such as annual reports of the company Apple, Inc., relevant statistical data, academic and business literature.

Besides, the reliable tools of information analysis applied in the TASGRAM system were used.

Which Knowledge and Qualities Are Needed for Strategy Creation?

The book provides a minimum set of knowledge for successful application of the TASGRAM system of strategy creation:

1. The importance of strategy for the company is demonstrated.
2. On the basis of theoretical postulates, empiric verification the answer to the question "What is strategy?" was provided.
3. The difference between business strategy and corporate strategy and their purposes is shown.
4. All stages of strategy creation with the help of the TASGRAM system are described.
5. The idea is given of the tools applied at each stage of strategy creation.
6. It is shown how information should be arranged for its visual presentation.

However, this is certainly not enough. Jack Welch noted that as CEO he got involved in everything: strategy, new products, sales, and the like (Welch and Welch, 2005). But it was the company's personnel that Jack Welch considered to be his main responsibility, as it was them who finally create and realize the strategy and develop new products (Welch and Welch, 2005).

Consequently, the skill of interaction with people, of creating a team united by the common goal and values, of motivating and inspiring the employees is the priority in the process of strategy creation. It is stated that a ticket to success in strategy creation and realization is effective interaction among the company's personnel (Hardina, 2002).

Besides, the presence of analytical skills, the ability of information operating enters in the foreground. It is impossible to conduct the PESTEL analysis, VRIO, and generally any analysis without a skill of analyzing information, making conclusions on the basis of analysis. In this, critical thinking plays the leading role.

In the process of strategy creation critical thinking means the skill to compare various facts, to find their strong and weak points.

The ability to operate information and critical thinking will allow understanding which solution will be beneficial for a client and which will not, because it is the client who will determine in the long run how successful the company's strategy was.

Such feature as creativity is also important. Hermann (1996:245) states that creativity *"is the ability to challenge assumptions, break boundaries, recognize patterns, see in new ways, make new connections, take risks, and seize upon chance when dealing with a problem"*.

It is creativity that will help to find not only a correct, but a unique solution, owing to which the company will be able to form a client proposition of the top value, as it was done by Steve Jobs with the help of a unique smartphone.

Of substantial importance will also be the knowledge in the project management sphere. PMI – Project Management institute (no data) defines Project management as *"the application of knowledge, skills, tools, and techniques to project activities to meet the project requirements"*.

In addition, strategy creation presumes the application of certain knowledge and skills to achieve economic value. Consequently, the approach to strategy from project management positions will enable more effective organization of its creation and realization.

Also, knowledge in the field of financial management, the ability to work with financial ratios are very important.

Not of minor importance is experience and subject knowledge. Miron Tribus, Dr. Deming's supporter and interpreter, the author of numerous research works emphasized that you can manage what you do not understand; but you cannot lead it (Neave, 1990). Bezos (2017) noted that when he was beginning his Amazon.com creation, he possessed the necessary knowledge corresponding to the highest standards on inventing, on customer care, and on hiring, but he knew nothing about the rational organization of operation activity. The necessary knowledge was obtained in the process of work and cooperation with colleagues. Today Amazon.com is one of the global leading companies. This example demonstrates that not only knowledge and experience are needed, but also their continuous development and improvement.

Therefore, owing to this chapter some recommendations were given as to the optimal application of the TASGRAM system, as well as concerns strategy creation.

5   Concluding Remarks

Peter Drucker (2008:128) emphasized that the main tasks of a strategy is to define how the business should operate at the moment and how we should prepare *"today's business for the future"*. The conducted work showed that the TASGRAM system meets these criteria completely and presents the answer to the basic question related to the company's strategy: "What is our business, and what should it be?"

1. By means of its business strategy the company determines the ways through which it generates economic value at present.
2. In the framework of corporate strategy the company will denote the ways of realizing the further economic value creation.

Thereat, the emphasis should be made on the fact that the company creates economic value due to full satisfaction or anticipation of the customers' requirements, but not due to its superiority over the competitors. Certainly, competition has not been cancelled. But the fact remains: today's business is mainly about the customers, but not about the competitors. When Steve Jobs and his team were working at the iPhone he was hardly thinking about his competitors, because there was no similar product on the market yet. However, as soon as the iPhone was introduced on the market, the companies which manufactured mobile phones copied the concept and entered the competitive fight with each other. But the iPhone was created with consideration to the customers' expectations as to innovative products; that is why Apple, Inc. took its confident leadership place in the industry. Steve Jobs noted that some people say: *"give the customers what they want, but that's not my approach. Our job is to figure out what they're going to want before they do"* (Smith, 2019).

So, the main secret of winning strategy lies in the company's ability to anticipate its customers' expectations, leaving its competitors far behind by doing this. Drucker (2008:82) remarks: "*Management must start with customer values and customer decisions as the basis for its strategy*".

Owing to the TASGRAM system, the definition of strategy can be presented, with consideration to the fact that strategy is a holistic process consisting of numerous elements. Thuswise, according to the TASGRAM system, strategy is:

1. Definition of the present and future ways of the company's development with the help of working out its business and corporate strategies.
2. Definition of strategic goals, actions, and risks which can influence the strategy realization.
3. Close attention to the key stakeholders and the analysis of their influence rate on the strategy realization.
4. Exercising of strategy realization monitoring.

Further on, the operational level follows, on which, on the basis of strategic goals and actions, the strategy realization is exercised, and the conversion of the obtained total net sales into net profit. Consequently, in the final sum the success of the company's actions aimed at the strategy creation on the operational level depends on whether the customers will receive an adequate value proposition and whether the company will receive economic value necessary for its development. Thuswise, the purpose of the following research is the creation of the optimal approach to organization of actions on strategy realization on the operational level, to working out the mechanism of the formation of customer value proposition. Due to such approach, the TASGRAM strategy system can be enforced by a new decision, presuming effective strategy realization on the operational level. This will enable business to organize the work on strategy formation in an optimal way, on the basis of verified methodologies of strategy creation and strategy realization.

References

Ackoff, Russel (1999), "A Lifetime of System Thinking", *Pegasus Communications*, 10(5), available at https://thesystemsthinker.com/wp-content/uploads/pdfs/100501pk.pdf, accessed 16 February 2020.

Adidas (2012), "Adidas Group at a Glance 2012", available at www.adidas-group.com/media/filer_public/2013/07/31/adidas_gb_2012_en_booklet_en.pdf, accessed 17 September 2020.

Adnan, Farooqui (2019), "Samsung Estimates a 56% Fall in Profit even as Apple Reimburses $684 Million", available at www.sammobile.com/news/samsung-56-fall-in-profit-apple-reimburses-684-million/, accessed 3 September 2020.

Agarwal, Rachit (2020), "15 Best iTunes Alternatives You Can Use", available at https://beebom.com/best-itunes-alternatives/, accessed 3 September 2020.

Agomuoh, Fionna (2018), "AI-powered Smartphones and the Features that Will Make You Want to Buy Them", available at www.businessinsider.com/ai-smartphones-artificial-intelligence-features-phones-2018-1, accessed 1 September 2020.

Aliekperov, Adyl (2021), "The Customer Experience Model", New York, NY: Routledge.

Alsadeq, Imad and Hakam, Tarek (2010), "Meet the New Project Manager – Mr. KPI". Paper presented at PMI® Global Congress 2010 – EMEA, Milan, Italy. Newtown Square, available at www.pmi.org/learning/library/project-managers-strategic-objectives-value-6827, accessed 31 January 2020.

Alsop, Thomas (2020), "Share of Households with a Computer at Home Worldwide from 2005 to 2019", available at www.statista.com/statistics/748551/worldwide-households-with-computer/, accessed 8 September 2020.

Amaro, Silvia (2020), "Apple Fined a Record $1.2 Billion by French Antitrust Authorities", available at www.cnbc.com/2020/03/16/apple-fined-1point2-billion-by-french-competition-authorities.html, accessed 1 September 2020.

Amazon (2009), "2009 Annual Report", available at https://s2.q4cdn.com/299287126/files/doc_financials/annual/AMZN_Annual-Report-2009-(final).pdf, accessed 14 February 2020.

Amazon (2018), "2018 Annual Report", available at https://ir.aboutamazon.com/static-files/0f9e36b1-7e1e-4b52-be17-145dc9d8b5ec, accessed 14 February 2020.

Amazon (2019a), "2019 Annual Report", available at https://s2.q4cdn.com/299287126/files/doc_financials/2020/ar/2019-Annual-Report.pdf, accessed 14 February 2020.

Amazon (2019b), "Prime Delivery Benefits You May not Know About", available at www.amazon.com/primeinsider/tips/all-pr-delivery-benefits.html, accessed 20 February 2020.

Amazon.com (no data, a), "Amazon Offers Refunds If Price Of Ordered Item Drops" available at https://sellercentral.amazon.com/forums/t/amazon-offers-refunds-if-price-of-ordered-item-drops/277465, accessed 20 August 2020.

Amazon.com (no data, b), "How to Get Started", available at www.amazon.com/b?ie=UTF8&node=16256994011, accessed 20 August 2020.

Amazon Services (no data), "Start Selling Online", available at https://services.amazon.com/services/soa-approval-category.html, accessed 19 February 2020. https://sellercentral.amazon.com/forums/t/amazon-offers-refunds-if-price-of-ordered-item-drops/277465/2

Ansoff, Igor. (1957), "Strategies for Diversification", *Harvard Business Review*, 35(5), 113–124v.

Apple, Inc. (2009), "FORM 10-K", available at www.sec.gov/Archives/edgar/data/320193/000119312509214859/d10k.htm, accessed 29 June 2020.

Apple, Inc. (2014), "FORM 10-K", available at www.annualreports.com/HostedData/AnnualReportArchive/a/NASDAQ_AAPL_2014.pdf, accessed 29 June 2020.

Apple, Inc. (2016), "Form 10-K", available at https://s2.q4cdn.com/470004039/files/doc_financials/2016/annual/10-K_2016_9.24.2016_-_as_filed.pdf, accessed 8 September 2020.

Apple, Inc. (2019a), "Environmental Responsibility Report", available at www.apple.com/environment/pdf/Apple_Environmental_Responsibility_Report_2019.pdf, accessed 1 September 2020.

Apple, Inc. (2019b), "FORM 10-K", available at https://investor.apple.com/investor-relations/default.aspx, accessed 29 June 2020.

Apple, Inc. (2019c), "Letter from Tim Cook to Apple Investors", available at www.apple.com/newsroom/2019/01/letter-from-tim-cook-to-apple-investors/, accessed 31 August 2020.

Apple, Inc. (2020), "Condensed Consolidated Statements of Operations (Unaudited)", available at https://s2.q4cdn.com/470004039/files/doc_financials/2020/q2/FY20_Q2_Consolidated_Financial_Statements.pdf, accessed 1 September 2020.

Apple, Inc. (no data, a), "Apple at Work", available at www.apple.com/business/, accessed 3 September 2020.

Apple, Inc. (no data,b), "Apple Authorized Distributor", available at www.apple.com/hk/en/buy/reseller/distributor.html, accessed 7 September 2020.

Apple, Inc. (no data,c), "Apple's COVID-19 Response", available at www.apple.com/newsroom/2020/03/apples-covid-19-response/, accessed 1 September 2020.

Apple, Inc. (no data,d), "iPhone 11 Pro", available at www.apple.com/us-hed/shop/buy-iphone/iphone-11-pro, accessed 31 August 2020.

Apple, Inc. (no data,e), "Shopping Help", available at www.apple.com/shop/help/iphone, accessed 7 September 2020.

Aten, Jason (2019), "Apple Is Now the Most Valuable Brand Ever, Thanks to This 1 Thing. (The Good News Is You Can Totally Do It Too)", available at www.inc.com/jason-aten/apple-is-now-most-valuable-brand-ever-thanks-to-this-1-thing-the-good-news-is-you-can-totally-do-it-too.html, accessed 31 August 2020.

Australian Government (2018), "Australian Entities and the EU General Data Protection Regulation (GDPR)", available at www.oaic.gov.au/privacy/guidance-and-advice/australian-entities-and-the-eu-general-data-protection-regulation/, accessed 2 September 2020.

Bailey, Michael , Johnston, Drew , Kuchler, Theresa et al. (2019), "Peer Effects in Product Adoption", available at www.nber.org/papers/w25843.pdf, accessed 7 September 2020.

Baldoni, John (2012), "Lead with Purpose: Giving Your Organization a Reason to Believe in Itself", New York, NY: AMACOM.

Bankmycell (no data), "How Many Smartphones Are the World?", available at www.bankmycell.com/blog/how-many-phones-are-in-the-world, accessed 8 September 2020.

Barboza, David (no data), "An iPhone's Journey, From the Factory Floor to the Retail Store" available at www.nytimes.com/2016/12/29/technology/iphone-china-apple-stores.html, accessed 3 September 2020.

Barnes, Matthew (2017), "What Customers Want in a New Flagship Smartphone", available at https://techmalak.com/what-customers-want-in-a-new-flagship-smartphone/#.Xu5C-2gzbIU, accessed 1 September 2020.

BCG.com (no data), "What Is the Growth Share Matrix?", available at www.bcg.com/about/our-history/growth-share-, accessed 3 September 2020.

Berry, Leonard (1995), "Relationship Marketing of Services-Growing Interest, Emerging Perspectives", *Journal of the Academy of Marketing Science*, (September, 1995), 23, 236–244.

Bershidsky, Leonid (2019), "Huawei Can Build a Fine Phone Without U.S. Parts", available at www.bloomberg.com/opinion/articles/2019-06-16/huawei-phones-made-under-u-s-ban-would-be-fine-not-innovative, accessed 1 September 2020.

Betz, Frederick (2016), "Strategic Thinking: A Comprehensive Guide", Bingley: Emerald Group Publishing.

Bezos, Jeffrey (letters 1997–2018), "1997–2018 Letters to Shareholders", available at https://ir.aboutamazon.com/annual-reports, accessed 14 February 2020.

Bezos, Jeffrey (1997), "1997 Letters to Shareholders", available at https://ir.aboutamazon.com/static-files/589ab7fe-9362-4823-a8e5-901f6d3a0f00, accessed 14 February 2020.

Bezos, Jeffrey (1998), "1998 Letters to Shareholders", available at https://ir.aboutamazon.com/static-files/4e153845-db22-4ea3-9876-e62b7935d05e, accessed 14 February 2020.

Bezos, Jeffrey (1999), "1999 Letters to Shareholders", available at https://ir.aboutamazon.com/static-files/35247dea-9cf4-46e3-9d8e-b501a1e41fee, accessed 14 February 2020.

Bezos, Jeffrey (2017), "2017 Letters to Shareholders", available at https://blog.aboutamazon.com/company-news/2017-letter-to-shareholders/, accessed 20 August 2020.

Bezos, Jeffrey (2018), "2018 Letters to Shareholders", available at https://ir.aboutamazon.com/static-files/4f64d0cd-12f2-4d6c-952e-bbed15ab1082, accessed 14 February 2020.

Blanchard, Ken (2007), "The Heart of a Leader: Insights on the Art of Influence", Colorado Springs, CO: David C. Cook.

Boston Consulting Group (2019), "The Most Innovative Companies 2019", available at https://image-src.bcg.com/Images/BCG-Most-Innovative-Companies-Mar-2019-R2_tcm9-215836.pdf, accessed 14 February 2020.

Browne, Ryan (2019), "Samsung and Apple are Losing Ground to Huawei because Their Phones are too Expensive, Research Shows", available at www.cnbc.com/2019/02/21/huawei-takes-market-share-from-apple-iphone-samsung-galaxy-gartner.html, accessed 31 August 2020.

Bryson, John (2004), "What to Do When Stakeholders Matter: A Guide to Stakeholder Identification and Analysis Techniques", *Public Management Review*, 6(1): 21–53. ISSN 1471–9037 print/ISSN 1471–9045. Online. Taylor & Francis Ltd.

Carman, Ashley (2018), "Samsung Introduces Its First Phone with a Triple-camera Setup", available at www.theverge.com/circuitbreaker/2018/9/20/17882238/samsung-galaxy-a7-phone-release-date-camera, accessed 31 August 2020.

Carrol, Archie and Buchholtz, Ann (2009), "Business & Society: Ethics and Stakeholder Management", Mason, OH: Cengage Learning.

Chen, Brian (2020), "What You Need to Know About 5G in 2020", available at www.nytimes.com/2020/01/08/technology/personaltech/5g-mobile-network.html?auth=login-facebook, accessed 1 September 2020.

Cipriani, Jason (2019), "Best Phones for 2019", available at www.zdnet.com/article/alternatives-to-apples-ecosystem-yes-there-is-a-way-out/, accessed 3 September,= 2020.

Cone Communications (2017), "CSR STUDY", available at www.conecomm.com/2017-cone-communications-csr-study-pdf, accessed 1 September 2020.

Consumer Policy Research Centre (2017), "Building Customer Trust A principles and practice guide", available at http://cprc.org.au/wp-content/uploads/CPRC_BCTR_WEB.pdf, accessed 20 October 2019.

Costello, Sam (2020), "Is Android or iPhone the Better Smartphone?", available at www.lifewire.com/iphone-vs-android-best-smartphone-2000309, accessed 3 September 2020.

Curac-Dahl (2019), "Data Privacy Laws in the United States and How They Affect Your Business", available at https://piwik.pro/blog/data-privacy-laws-united-states/#ccpa, accessed 2 September 2020.

da-Silva, Adolphine (2016), "Define your Business Goal", San-Francisco, CA: ETATS-UNITS.

Deloitte (2013), "Exploring Strategic Risk", available at www2.deloitte.com/content/dam/Deloitte/global/Documents/Governance-Risk-Compliance/dttl-grc-exploring-strategic-risk.pdf, accessed 24 October 2020.

Dholakia, Utpal (2016), "A Quick Guide to Value-Based Pricing", available at https://hbr.org/2016/08/a-quick-guide-to-value-based-pricing, accessed 30 January 2020.

Digg (2018), "The Price of Every iPhone, Adjusted for Inflation", available at https://digg.com/2018/iphone-prices, accessed 1 September 2020.

Disney (2019) "Annual Financial Report", available at https://thewaltdisneycompany.com/app/uploads/2020/01/2019-Annual-Report.pdf, accessed 1 September 2020.

Drucker, Jesse and Bowers, Simon (2019), [*New York Times*], "After a Tax Crackdown, Apple Found a New Shelter for Its Profits", available at www.nytimes.com/2017/11/06/world/apple-taxes-jersey.html, accessed 1 September 2019.

Drucker, Peter (2008), "Management", revised edition, Harper Collins. E-book.

Elgan, Mike (2011), "What Android Fans Think of iPhone Users", available at https://bit.ly/3dqYzXe, accessed 7 September 2020.

Encyclopedia Britannica (2019), "iPhone Electronic Device", available at www.britannica.com/technology/iPhone, accessed 29 June 2020.

Enenkel, Karl et al. (2017), "Intersections", Leiden/Boston: Brill.

Epstein, Marc and Buhovac, Adriana (2006), "The Reporting of Organizational Risks for Internal and External Decision-Making", published by The Society of Management Accountants of Canada and The American Institute of Certified Public Accountants.

Estrin, James (2015), "Kodak's First Digital Moment", available at https://lens.blogs.nytimes.com/2015/08/12/kodaks-first-digital-moment/, accessed 23 September 2020.

Euronews (2020), "Coronavirus Second Wave? Which Countries in Europe Are Experiencing a Resurgence of Cases?", available at www.euronews.com/2020/07/31/is-europe-having-a-covid-19-second-wave-country-by-country-breakdown, accessed 1 September 2020.

Express (2017), "Revealed: Top Uses of Our Smartphones – and Calling Doesn't even Make the List", available at www.express.co.uk/life-style/science-technology/778572/Smartphone-phone-common-reason-use-call, accessed 7 September 2020.

Fao.org (no data), "Stakeholder Analysis", available at www.fao.org/elearning/course/FK/en/pdf/trainerresources/PG_StakeHolder.pdf, accessed 29 June 2020.

Fader, Peter and Sarah, Toms (2018), "The Customer Centricity Playbook", Philadelphia, PA: Wharton Digital Press.

Ferrell, Odies C. and Hartline, Michael (2008), "Marketing Strategy", Mason, OH: Thomson South Western.

Fingas, Jon (2013), "The Ever-expanding Smartphone Screen: How Supersized Became Everyday", available at www.engadget.com/2013-03-01-the-ever-expanding-smartphone-screen.html, accessed 31 August 2020.

Fingas, Roger (2019), "iPhone's Global Market Share Dips to 10.1% Amid Rise of Samsung & Chinese Brands", available at https://appleinsider.com/articles/19/07/31/iphones-global-marketshare-dips-to-101-amid-rise-of-samsung-chinese-brands, accessed 31 August 2020.

Fisher, Alec and Scriven, Michael (1997), "Critical Thinking. Its Definition and Assessment", University of East Anglia, Centre for Research in Critical, Norwich, UK.

Fisk, Raymond; Grove, Stephen and John, Joby (2014), "Services Marketing Interactive Approach", Mason, OH: South-Wester, Cengage Learning.

Fortune (2020), "Fortune 500", available at https://fortune.com/fortune500/, accessed 29 June 2020.

Freeman, Edward (2010), "Strategic Management: A Stakeholder Approach", Cambridge: Cambridge University Press.

Freeman, Edward (2016), "The New Story of Business: Towards a More Responsible Capitalism", a public lecture, available at https://onlinelibrary.wiley.com/doi/abs/10.1111/basr.12123, accessed 6 January 2020.

Freeman, Edward and McVea, John (2001), Working Paper No. 01-02, Darden Graduate School of Business Administration, University of Virginia, available at www.researchgate.net/publication/228320877_A_Stakeholder_Approach_to_Strategic_Management, accessed 31 August 2020.

Gad, Thomas (2016), "Customer Experience Branding: Driving Engagement Through Surprise and Innovation", London: Kogan Page.

Galetto, Molly (2017), "Customer Retention Marketing: 50 Expert Tips and Insights on Customer Retention Marketing Trends, Tactics and Best Practice Strategies", available at www.ngdata.com/customer-retention-marketing-strategies/, accessed 15 September 2020.

Gallo, Amy (2014), "The Value of Keeping the Right Customers", available at https://hbr.org/2014/10/the-value-of-keeping-the-right-customers, accessed 15 October 2020.

Gartenberg, Chaim (2017), "Samsung's component division will make more money off the iPhone X than the Galaxy S8", available at www.theverge.com/circuitbreaker/2017/10/2/16404430/samsung-iphone-x-galaxy-s8-screen-components-money-revenue-display, accessed 3 September 2020.

Gartenberg, Chaim (2019), "For Customers Who Want the 'Most Sophisticated Technology", available at www.theverge.com/2019/9/10/20851377/iphone-11-pro-max-release-date-camera-features-specs-announcement-apple, accessed 31 August 2020.

Gartner (2016), "Gartner Says Worldwide Smartphone Sales Grew 9.7 Percent in Fourth Quarter of 2015", available at https://gtnr.it/31zMitN, accessed 3 September 2020.

Gartner (2020), "Gartner Says Global Smartphone Sales Fell Slightly in the Fourth Quarter of 2019", available at www.gartner.com/en/newsroom/press-releases/2020-03-03-gartner-says-global-smartphone-sales-fell-slightly-in, accessed 3 September 2020.

General Electric (2017), "GE Additive Opens Customer Experience Center in Munich", available at www.genewsroom.com/press-releases/ge-additive-opens-customer-experience-center-munich, accessed 6 December 2020.

General Electric (2019), "2019 Annual Report", available at www.ge.com/investor-relations/annual-report, accessed 29 June 2020.

General Electric (2020), "2020 Notice of Annual Meeting and Proxy Statement", available at www.sec.gov/Archives/edgar/data/40545/000120677420000797/ge_courtesy-pdf.pdf, accessed 12 August 2020.

Ghaffary, Shirin (2018), "Watch: Apple CEO Tim Cook Explains Why 'Privacy Is a Human Right'", available at www.vox.com/2018/4/6/17197754/watch-apple-ceo-tim-cook-msnbc, accessed 7 September 2020.

Grant, Robert and Jordan, Judith (2016), "Foundations of Strategy", London: Wiley.

GSM Arena (2020), "Apple May Reportedly Move 20% of iPhone Production from China to India", available at www.gsmarena.com/apple_to_become_indias_largest_exporter_may_reportedly_move_20_of_iphone_production_from_china_to_in-news-43133.php, accessed 3 September 2020.

Gov.uk (no data), "Data Protection" available at www.gov.uk/data-protection, accessed 2 September 2020.

Hansen, Drew (2013), "Myth Busted: Steve Jobs Did Listen to Customers", available at www.forbes.com/sites/drewhansen/2013/12/19/myth-busted-steve-jobs-did-listen-to-customers/#59681d4387f3, accessed 30 January 2020.

Hardina, Donna (2002), "Analytical Skills for Community Organization Practice", New York, NY: Columbia University Press.

Haselton, Todd (2017), "Here's Why People Keep Buying Apple Products", available at www.cnbc.com/2017/05/01/why-people-keep-buying-apple-products.html, accessed 3 September 2020.

He, Laura (2020), "China's Economy Is Still Struggling to Recover from the Pandemic", available at https://edition.cnn.com/2020/06/08/economy/china-trade-economy-intl-hnk/index.html, accessed 1 September 2020.

Hill, Simon (2020), "Android vs. iOS: Which Smartphone Platform is the Best?", available at www.digitaltrends.com/mobile/android-vs-ios/, accessed 3 September 2020.

Hilton (2019), "Annual Report", available at https://sec.report/Document/0001585689-20-000013/, accessed 1 September 2020.

Hindsley, Grant (2020), "The Lost Month: How a Failure to Test Blinded the U.S. to Covid-19", available at www.nytimes.com/2020/03/28/us/testing-coronavirus-pandemic.html, accessed 23 September 2020.

Hixon, Todd (2014), "What Kind Of Person Prefers An iPhone? What Kind Of Person Prefers An iPhone?" available at www.forbes.com/sites/toddhixon/2014/04/10/what-kind-of-person-prefers-an-iphone/#33e2333bd1b0, accessed 7 September 2020.

Huawei Company (2019), "Annual Report", available at www-file.huawei.com/
-/media/corporate/pdf/annual-report/annual_report_2019_en.pdf?la=en,
accessed 1 September 2019.

Huawei (no data,a), "Green World", available at www.huawei.com/en/sustain-
ability/environment-protect/green_world, accessed 1 September 2020.

Huawei (no data,b), "Intelligent Store Management of Huawei Retail Stores
Intelligent Store Management of Huawei Retail Stores", available at
https://e.huawei.com/ua/case-studies/global/2018/201809281048, accessed 3
September 2020.

Interbrand (2019a), "01 Apple", available at www.interbrand.com/best-brands/
best-global-brands/2019/ranking/apple/, accessed 31 August 2020.

Interbrand (2019b), "Best Global Brands 2019 Rankings", available at www.
interbrand.com/best-brands/best-global-brands/2019/ranking/, accessed 31
August 2020.

Interbrand (no data), "Methodology", available at www.interbrand.com/
best-brands/best-global-brands/methodology/#brand_strength, accessed 7
September 2020.

Ismail, Adam (2019), "OnePlus 7T vs. iPhone 11: Battle of the Affordable
Flagships", available at www.tomsguide.com/face-off/oneplus-7t-vs-iphone-
11, accessed 3 September 2020.

Jackson, Michael (2003), "Systems Thinking: Creative Holism for Managers",
Chichester: John Wiley & Sons Ltd.

Johanson, Johny and Carlson, Kurt (2015), "Contemporary Brand
Management", Thousands Oaks, CA: Sage.

Johnson, Gerry; Scholes, Kevan and Whittington, Richard (2008), "Exploring
Corporate Strategy", Harlow: Pearson Education Limited.

J.D. Power (2017), "Smartphone Satisfaction Higher as Customer Homes
Become More Connected, J.D. Power Finds", available at, www.
constructdigital.com/insight/why-are-people-are-buying-the-new-iphones,
accessed 7 September 2020.

Kidman, Alex and Jager, Chris (2020), "Best iPhone Alternatives for 2020: The
Phones that Give Apple a Serious Run for Its Money", available at www.
finder.com.au/best-iphone-alternatives, accessed 3 September 2020.

Kotler, Philip and Keller, Kevin (2016), "Marketing Management", Edinburgh,
UK: Pearson Education.

Kumar, Piyush (1999), "The Impact of Long-Term Client Relationships on
the Performance of Business Service Firms", available at http://citeseerx.
ist.psu.edu/viewdoc/download?doi=10.1.1.197.9643&rep=rep1&type=pdf,
accessed 20 October 2019.

Latham, Ann (2017), "What the Heck Is a Strategy Anyway?", available at
www.forbes.com/sites/annlatham/2017/10/29/what-the-heck-is-a-strategy-
anyway/#13a9b3f67ed8, accessed 29 June 2020.

Lee, Jenifer (no data), "Is the Customer Always Right? How Consumers
Can Help Drive Innovation", available at www2.deloitte.com/ca/en/pages/
consumer-business/articles/consumer-driven-innovation.html#, accessed 3
September 2020.

Lehrer, Jeff (2020), "Top 5 Forward Thinking Trends for the Modern Enterprise", available at www.forbes.com/sites/sap/2020/06/18/top-5-forward-thinking-trends-for-the-modern-enterprise/#578ce731737f, accessed 7 September 2020.

Lewis, Robin (2014), "How Apple Neurologically Hooked Its Customers", available at www.forbes.com/sites/robinlewis/2014/09/02/how-apple-neurologically-hooked-its-customers/#708e05e4ff00, accessed 30 January 2020.

Maley, Claude (2012). "Project Management Concepts, Methods, and Techniques", London: CRC Press.

Maslow, Abraham (1970), "Motivation and Personality", Harper & Row Publishers.

Matyszczyk, Chris (2018), "Why Do People Want a New iPhone? This Research Gives a Fascinating Clue", available at www.tomsguide.com/face-off/iphone-11-pro-vs-galaxy-s10, accessed 2 September 2020.

McGarry, Caitlin (2020), "iPhone 11 Pro vs. Samsung Galaxy S10: Which flagship phone should you buy?", available at www.forbes.com/sites/robinlewis/2014/09/02/how-apple-neurologically-hooked-its-customers/#708e05e4ff00, accessed 30 January 2021.

McKeown, Max (2012:21), "The strategy book", Harlow: Pearson.

Mendelow, A. L. (1981), "Environmental Scanning: The Impact of the Stakeholder Concept", *Proceedings from the Second International Conference on Information Systems*, 407–418, Cambridge, MA.

Mercer (no data), "'The Global Risks Report 2020'", available at www.mercer.com/content/dam/mercer/attachments/global/gl-2020-the-global-risks-report-2020.pdf., accessed 23 September, 2020.

Merchant, Brian (2017), "The One Device: The Secret History of the iPhone", New York, NY: Little, Brown and Company.

Mishra, Varun (2019), "Premium Smartphone Market Collapses 8% in Q1 2019, After Apple Shipments Drop 20%", available at www.counterpointresearch.com/premium-smartphone-market-collapses-8-q1-2019-apple-shipments-drop-20/", accessed 31 August, 2020.

Moorhead, Patrick (2019), "Who Are Apple's iPhone Contract Manufacturers?", available at www.forbes.com/sites/patrickmoorhead/2019/04/13/who-are-apples-iphone-contract-manufacturers/#18c4798b4e6d., accessed 6 January, 2020.

Moorman, Christine (2012), "Myth Busted: Steve Jobs Did Listen To Customers", available at www.forbes.com/sites/christinemoorman/2012/07/10/why-apple-is-a-great-marketer/#30efcc37297d, accessed 30 January, 2020.

Moren, Dan (2020), "4 places where Apple can improve its integration of hardware, software, and services", available at www.macworld.com/article/3516134/4-places-where-apple-can-improve-its-integration-of-hardware-software-and-services.html, accessed 3 September, 2020.

Morgan, Clancy and Houston, Jack (2019), "Why Apple products are so expensive", available at www.businessinsider.com/why-apple-products-are-so-expensive-iphone-macbook-2019-11, accessed 3 September, 2020.

National Law Review (2020), "Federal Privacy Legislation Update: Consumer Data Privacy and Security Act of 2020" available at www.natlawreview. com/article/federal-privacy-legislation-update-consumer-data-privacy-and-security-act-2020, accessed 2 September 2020.

Neave, Henry (1990), "The Deming Dimension", Knoxville, TN: SPC Press.

Nicholas, John and Steyn, Herman (2012), "Project Management for Engineering, Business and Technology", Oxon: Routledge.

Nielson, Samantha (2014), "Apple's Premium Pricing Strategy and Product Differentiation", available https://finance.yahoo.com/news/apple-premium-pricing-strategy-product-191247308.html, accessed 30 January 2020.

Norton (no data), "Android vs. iOS: Which Is More Secure?" available at https://nr.tn/3mc3wXD, accessed 7 September 2020.

Norton, Robert and Kaplan, David (2001), "The Strategy-focused Organization: How Balanced Scorecard Companies Thrive in the New Business Environment", Boston: Harward Business School Press.

Norton, Robert and Kaplan, David (2005), "The Office of Strategy Management", available at https://hbr.org/2005/10/the-office-of-strategy-management%20, accessed 7 September 2020.

O'Dea, S. (2020a), "Global Smartphone Shipments in February 2019 and February 2020", available at www.statista.com/statistics/1106603/global-smartphone-shipments-coronavirus-covid-19/, accessed 1 September 2020.

O'Dea, S. (2020b), "Number of Apple iPhone Devices in Use in the U.S., China and the Rest of the World in 2017", available at www.statista.com/statistics/755625/iphones-in-use-in-us-china-and-rest-of-the-world/, accessed 7 September 2020.

O'Dea, S. (2020c), "Share of Global Smartphone Shipments by Operating System from 2014 to 2023", available at https://bit.ly/3wk2ePh, accessed 3 September 2020.

O'Hara, Susan and Levin, Ginger (2000), "Using Metrics to Demonstrate the Value of Project Management". Paper presented at Project Management Institute Annual Seminars & Symposium, Houston, TX. Newtown Square, available at www.pmi.org/learning/library/metrics-demonstrate-value-project-management-485, accessed 31 January 2020.

Official Journal of the European Union (2016), "Regulations", available at https://eur-lex.europa.eu/legal-content/EN/TXT/PDF/?uri=CELEX:32016R0679, accessed 2 September 2020.

Olson, Aaron and Simerson, Keith (2015), "Leading with Strategic Thinking", Hoboken, New Jersey: Wiley.

Oxfam America (2016), "Broken at the Top", available at www.oxfamamerica.org/static/media/files/Broken_at_the_Top_FINAL_EMBARGOED_4.12.2016.pdf, accessed 1 September 2019.

Passenheim, Olaf (2014), "Project Management", available at bookboon.com, accessed 23 December 2019.

Pathak, Tarun (2019a), "Apple Maintains Lead in Premium Smartphone Segment, OnePlus Enters Top Five Brands for the First Time in 2018", available at https://bit.ly/2PotbAA., accessed 31 August 2020.

Pathak, Tarun (2019b), "OnePlus Enters Top Five Brands for the First Time in 2018", available at www.counterpointresearch.com/apple-maintains-lead-premium-smartphone-segment-oneplus-enters-top-five-brands-first-time-2018/, accessed 31 August 2020.

Pemberton, Chris (2018), "Key Findings from the Gartner Customer Experience Survey", available at www.gartner.com/en/marketing/insights/articles/key-findings-from-the-gartner-customer-experience-survey, accessed 20 October 2019.

Peng, Mike (2009), "Global Strategy", Mason, OH: Cengage Learning.

Pidun, Ulrich (2019), "Corporate Strategy: Theory and Practice", Wiesbaden: Springer.

PMI – Project Management Institute (no data), "What is Project Management?", available at www.pmi.org/about/learn-about-pmi/what-is-project-management, accessed 23 September 2020.

Polonsky, Michael Jay and Rosenberger, Philip (2001), "Reevaluating Green Marketing: A Strategic Approach", *Business Horizons*, (September–October, 2001), 44(5), 1–30.

Porter, Michael (1996), "What is Strategy", *Harvard Business Review*, 74(6), 61–78.

Porter, Michael (1998), "Competitive Strategy", New York, NY: Free Press.

Porter, Michael (2008), "Competitive Strategy", New York, NY: Free Press.

Porter, Michael (2014), "What Is Strategy", available at www.youtube.com/watch?v=Zq9-JT8moU4, accessed 31 August 2020.

Porter, Michael (2015), "Michael Porter: Aligning Strategy & Project", available at www.youtube.com/watch?v=CKcSzH1SvCk, accessed 29 June 2020.

Profitero (2018), "Amazon Maintains Major Price Lead Over Other Online Retailers" available at www.profitero.com/press-release/amazon-maintains-major-price-lead-over-other-online-retailers/, accessed 20 August 2020.

Pruschkowski, Martin (2015), "The BCG Matrix and its Support of Management Decision Making", Nuremberg: Grin.

PWC (2020), "Top Policy Trends 2020: Data Privacy", available at www.pwc.com/us/en/library/risk-regulatory/strategic-policy/top-policy-trends/data-privacy.html, accessed 2 September 2020.

Ramage, Magnus and Shipp, Karen (2009), "Systems Thinkers", Heidelberg: Springer.

Rattner, Nate and Miller, Hannah (2020), "Here are Five Charts Illustrating the U.S. Economic Recovery amid the Coronavirus Pandemic", available at www.cnbc.com/2020/06/28/here-are-five-charts-illustrating-the-us-economic-recovery-amid-the-coronavirus-pandemic.html, accessed 1 September 2020.

Reichheld, Fred (2001), "Prescription for Cutting Costs" available at www2.bain.com/Images/BB_Prescription_cutting_costs.pdf, accessed 23 October 2019.

Reisenger, Don (2018), "Why Apple Will Keep Most iPhone Production in China Despite Tariff Threat", available at https://fortune.com/2019/06/13/apple-iphone-china-production/, accessed 3 September 2020.

Reisenger, Don (2019), "Apple's Wearables Could Be a $100 Billion Business, Analyst Says", available at https://fortune.com/2019/12/11/apples-wearables-100-billion-business-analyst-says/, accessed 3 September 2020.

Reuters (2020a), "German Economy Gradually Recovering after Pandemic Slump: Ifo", available at www.reuters.com/article/us-health-coronavirus-germany-economy/german-economy-gradually-recovering-after-pandemic-slump-ifo-idUSKBN2424W1, accessed 1 September 2020.

Reuters (2020b), "Timeline: Key Dates in the U.S.–China Trade War", available at www.reuters.com/article/us-usa-trade-china-timeline/timeline-key-dates-in-the-u-s-china-trade-war-idUSKBN1ZE1AA, accessed 1 September 2020.

Salisbury, Ian (2018), "Use These 10 Products? If So, You're Probably Wealthy", available at https://finance.yahoo.com/news/10-products-apos-wealthy-171541021.html, accessed 7 September 2020.

Santangelo, John James (2013), "Setting Goals – Quick & Easy Worksheet, Theory and SMART Goals!", publisher: John James Santangelo C. Ht.

Samsung (2015), "5 Reasons the Galaxy Note 5 is 'Phabulous' for Business", available at https://insights.samsung.com/2015/08/13/5-reasons-the-galaxy-note-5-is-phabulous-for-business/, accessed 31 August 2020.

Samsung (2016), "Business Report", available at https://images.samsung.com/is/content/samsung/p5/global/ir/docs/170331_2016_Business_Report_vF.pdf, accessed 20 October 2019.

Samsung (2017), "Samsung Electronics Sustainability Report", available at www.samsung.com/us/smg/content/dam/samsung/us/aboutsamsung/2017/Samsung_Electronics_Sustainability_Report-2017.pdf, accessed 20 October 2019.

Samsung (2019), "2019 Business Report", available at https://images.samsung.com/is/content/samsung/p5/global/ir/docs/2019_Business_Report.pdf, accessed 13 December 2020.

Samsung (no data, a), "Galaxy Store", available at www.samsung.com/us/explore/samsung-galaxy-apps, accessed 3 September 2020.

Samsung (no data, b), "Samsung Experience Store", available at www.samsung.com/us/samsung-experience-store/locations/, accessed 3 September 2020.

Samsung Company (no data), "Galaxy S10" available at www.samsung.com/us/mobile/galaxy-s10/, accessed 31 August 2020.

Samsung Newsroom (2017), "Applying Samsung's Innovative Spirit to Eco-Friendly Product Design", available at https://news.samsung.com/global/applying-samsungs-innovative-spirit-to-eco-friendly-product-design, accessed 1 September 2020.

Schneiders, Sasha (2011), "Apple's Secret of Success – Traditional Marketing Vs. Cult Marketing", Hamburg: Diplomica Verlag.

Sheetz, Michael (2020), "Amazon Will Invest over $10 Billion in Its Satellite Internet Network after Receiving FCC Authorization", available at www.cnbc.com/2020/07/30/fcc-authorizes-amazon-to-build-kuiper-satellite-internet-network.html, accessed 1 September 2020.

Smith, Dave (2019), "What Everyone Gets Wrong about This Famous Steve Jobs Quote, According to Lyft's Design Boss", available at www.businessinsider.com/steve-jobs-quote-misunderstood-katie-dill-2019-4, accessed 23 September 2020.

Snouwaert, Jessica (2020), "Coronavirus is Pushing Apple's iPhone Makers to Find New Manufacturing Frontiers Outside of China", available at www.businessinsider.com/apple-iphone-manufacturers-look-outside-of-china-amid-coronavirus-2020-3, accessed 3 September 2020.

Spence, Ewan (2019), "Latest iPhone 11 Details Confirms Disappointing Lack of Ideas", available at www.forbes.com/sites/ewanspence/2019/06/24/apple-iphone-upgrade-iphone-xs-max-iphone-xr-new-leak-rumor/#7a9a62a85012, accessed 8 September 2020.

Spoonauer, Mark (2019), "10 Reasons the iPhone Beats Android", available at www.tomsguide.com/us/iphone-is-better-than-android,news-21307.html, accessed 7 September 2020.

Stat counter (2020), "Desktop vs Mobile vs Tablet Market Share United States Of America Desktop vs Mobile vs Tablet Market Share in United States Of America", available at https://gs.statcounter.com/platform-market-share/desktop-mobile-tablet/united-states-of-america, accessed 9 September 2020.

Statista (2013), "Share of Android vs iPhone Mobile Owners in the US as of May 2013, by Education Level", available at www.statista.com/statistics/271229/anroid-vs-iphone-mobile-owners-education-level-us/, accessed 7 September 2020.

Stevenson, William (2015), "Operations Management" (McGraw-Hill Series in Operations and Decision Sciences) 12th Edition, Kindle Edition, Haddenham: Folens Limited.

Straubhaar, Joseph and LaRose, Robert (2015), "Media Now: Understanding Media, Culture, and Technology", Boston, MA: Cengage Learning.

Strupczewski, Jan (2020), "Explainer: How the EU Can Finance Economic Recovery after the COVID-19 Pandemic", available at www.reuters.com/article/us-health-coronavirus-eu-recovery-explai/explainer-how-the-eu-can-finance-economic-recovery-after-the-covid-19-pandemic-idUSKCN21X2BU, accessed 1 September 2020.

Sutherland, Jonathan and Canwell, Diane (2008), "AS Essential Business Studies for AQA", Haddenham: Folens Limited.

Tankovska, H. (2020a), "Global Research & Development Expenditure at Samsung Electronics between 2009 and 2019", available at www.statista.com/statistics/236924/samsung-electronics-research-and-development-expenditure/, accessed 13 December 2020.

Tankovska, H. (2020b), "TV Unit Sales Worldwide 2012–2017", available at www.statista.com/statistics/461316/global-tv-unit-sales/, accessed 15 September 2020.

Technavio (2019), "Top 10 Largest Smartphone Companies in the World 2019", available at https://blog.technavio.com/blog/top-10-largest-smartphone-companies, accessed 3 September 2020.

Todorovich, Milan and Bakir, Ali (2016), "Rethinking Strategy for Creative Industries: Innovation and Interaction", New York, NY: Routledge.

Tracy, John (2002), "The Fast Forward MBA in Finance", New York: John Willey and sons, Inc.

Veber, Max (1964), "The Theory of Social and Economic Organization", New York, NY: The Free Press.

Walmart, Inc (2020), "2020 Annual Report", available at https://s2.q4cdn.com/056532643/files/doc_financials/2020/ar/Walmart_2020_Annual_Report.pdf, accessed 12 August 2020.

Waterson, Jim (2020), "Amazon to Cut Price of Its ebooks to Reflect Removal of VAT" available at www.theguardian.com/books/2020/apr/30/amazon-to-cut-price-of-its-ebooks-to-reflect-removal-of-vat, accessed 20 August 2020.

Watson, Amy (2019), "Number of TV Households Worldwide 2010–2018", available at www.statista.com/statistics/268695/number-of-tv-households-worldwide/, accessed 15 September 2020.

Weinstein, Art and Ellison, Hank (2012), "Superior Customer Value: Strategies for Winning and Retaining Customers", Boca Raton, FL: CRC Press, Taylor and Francis.

Welch, Jack and Welch, Suzi (2005), "Winning", Harper Collins, Colorado Springs, CO: David Cook.

Whirlpool (2019), "2019 Annual Report", available at https://investors.whirlpoolcorp.com/financial-information/annual-reports-and-proxy-statements/default.aspx, accessed 29 June 2020.

Whitley, Margaret (2006), "Leadership and the New Science: Discovering Order in a Chaotic World", San Francisco, California: Barret–Koehler Publishers, Inc.

Williams, Rhiannon (2019), "How the iPhone Has Evolved in Size, from the Very First to the iPhone SE (2020)", available at https://inews.co.uk/news/technology/how-the-iphone-has-evolved-in-size-since-2007-got-bigger/, accessed 31 August 2020.

Wolverton, Troy (2019), "Apple's $24 Billion Wearables Segment is Now Almost as Big as Its Mac Business", available at www.businessinsider.com/apples-wearables-segment-now-almost-as-big-as-mac-business-2019-10, accessed 3 September 2020.

Wootton, Simon and Horne, Terry (2003), "Strategic Thinking: A Step-by-step Approach to Strategy Strategic Thinking: A Step-by-step Approach to Strategy", London: Kogan Page, Ltd.

World Bank (no data), "GDP Per Capita (Current US$)", available at https://data.worldbank.org/indicator/NY.GDP.PCAP.CD, accessed 1 September 2020.

World Economic Forum (2020), "The Global Risks Report 2020" available at www3.weforum.org/docs/WEF_Global_Risk_Report_2020.pdf, accessed 23 September 2020.

XIAOMI (2018), "Annual Report", available at https://i01.appmifile.com/ webfile/globalweb/company/ir/announcement_us/2018_ANNUAL_ REPORT.pdf, accessed 12 September 2020.

Zanoni, Andrea Beretta (2012), "Strategic Analysis: Processes and Tools", London: Routledge.

Zorfas, Alan and Leemon, Daniel (2016), [*Forbes*] "An Emotional Connection Matters More than Customer Satisfaction", available at https://hbr.org/2016/ 08/an-emotional-connection-matters-more-than-customer-satisfaction, accessed 30 January 2020.

Index

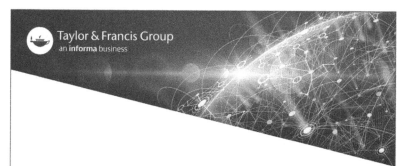